LITERARY ESSAYS

Literary Essays

by
JEAN-PAUL SARTRE

THE WISDOM LIBRARY

A DIVISION OF
PHILOSOPHICAL LIBRARY
New York

Published, 1957, by Philosophical Library, Inc.
15 East 40 Street, New York, N. Y.

Manufactured in the United States of America

CONTENTS

* Note: Camus' *The Outsider* was published in the U. S. under the title of *The Stranger*.

I

François Mauriac and Freedom

THE novel does not present things, but rather their signs.[1]
How, with these mere signs, these words that are *indications* in a vacuum, are we to build a world that holds together?
How does Stavrogin come alive? It would be an error to think
that he draws his life from my imagination. When we muse
over words, they beget images, but when I read, I am not
musing; I am deciphering. I do not imagine Stavrogin; I wait
for him; I wait expectantly for his acts, for the end of his
adventure.

The thick substance I brew as I read *The Possessed* is my
own expectancy, my own time. For a book is either a mere
stack of dry leaves or else a great form in motion, in other words,
the act of reading. The novelist takes hold of this movement,
guides and inflects it, makes of it the stuff of his characters.
A novel is a series of readings, of little parasitic lives, none of
them longer than a dance. It swells and feeds on the reader's
time. But in order for the duration of my impatience and
ignorance to be caught and then moulded and finally presented
to me as the flesh of these creatures of invention, the novelist
must know how to draw it into the trap, how to hollow out in
his book, by means of the signs at his disposal, a time resembling
my own, one in which the future does not exist. If I suspect
that the hero's future actions are determined in advance by
heredity, social influence or some other mechanism, my own
time ebbs back into me; there remains only myself, reading
and persisting, confronted by a static book. Do you want your
characters to live? See to it that they are free.

It is not a matter of defining passions and unpredictable
acts, still less of explaining them (in novels, even the best

[1] The observations in the present essay might also have been based on
M. Mauriac's more recent works, such as *Maimona* or *Plongées*. But his
particular purpose in writing *La Fin de la Nuit* was to treat the problem of
freedom. That is why I prefer to draw my examples from this book.

psychological analyses have a mouldy smell), but rather of *presenting* them. Neither you nor I know what Rogogine is going to do. I know that he is going to see his guilty mistress again, but I cannot tell whether he will control himself or whether his anger will drive him to murder; he is free. I slip into his skin, and there he is, awaiting himself with my waiting. He is afraid of himself, *inside me*; he is alive.

It occurred to me, as I was about to begin *La Fin de la Nuit*, that Christian writers, by the very nature of their belief, have the kind of mentality best suited to the writing of novels. The religious man is free. The supreme forbearance of the Catholic may irritate us, because it is an acquired thing. If he is a novelist, it is a great advantage. The fictional and the Christian man, who are both centres of indeterminacy, do have characters, but only in order to escape from them. They are free, above and beyond their natures, and if they succumb to their natures, here again, they do so freely. They may get caught up in psychological machinery, but they themselves are never mechanical.

Even the Christian conception of sin corresponds to one of the principles of the writing of fiction. The Christian sins, and the hero of the novel must err. If the existence of the error—which cannot be effaced and which must be redeemed—does not reveal to the reader the irreversibility of time, the substantial duration of the work of art lacks the urgency that gives it its necessity and cruelty. Thus, Dostoevsky was a Christian novelist. Not a novelist and a Christian, as Pasteur was a Christian *and* a scientist, but a novelist in the service of Christ.

M. Mauriac is also a Christian novelist, and his book, *La Fin de la Nuit*, tries to penetrate to the inmost depths of a woman's freedom. He tells us in his preface that he is trying to depict "the power accorded to creatures who have all the odds against them, the power to say *no* to the law that beats them down". Here we touch the heart of the art of fiction and the heart of faith. Nevertheless, I must admit that the book has disappointed me. Not for a moment was I taken in, never did I forget *my* time; I went on existing, I felt myself living. Occasionally I yawned. Now and then I said to myself, "Well done." I thought more often of M. Mauriac than of Thérèse Desqueyroux—of

M. Mauriac, subtle, sensitive and narrow, with his immodest discretion, his intermittent good will, his nervous pathos, his bitter and fumbling poetry, his pinched style, his sudden vulgarity. Why was I unable to forget him or myself? And what had become of this Christian predisposition for the novel? We must go back to the question of freedom. What are the processes by which M. Mauriac reveals to us the freedom he has conferred upon his heroine?

Thérèse Desqueyroux struggles against her destiny. Well and good. There are thus two elements in her make-up. One part of her is entirely an element of Nature; we can say this of her as we would of a stone or log. But another whole side of her defies description or definition, because it is simply an absence. If freedom accepts Nature, the reign of fatality begins. If it rejects and resists it, Thérèse Desqueyroux is free, free to say no, or free, at least, not to say yes. ("All that is asked of them is that they not resign themselves to darkness.") This is Cartesian freedom, infinite, formless, nameless and without destiny, "forever starting anew", whose only power is that of sanction, but which is sovereign because it can refuse sanction. There it is—at least as we see it in the preface. Do we find it in the novel?

The first thing to be said is that this suspensive will seems more tragic than novelistic. Thérèse's oscillations between the impulses of her nature and the action of her will are reminiscent of Rotrou's stanzas. The real conflict in a novel is rather between freedom and itself. In Dostoevsky, freedom is poisoned at its very source. It gets tangled up in the very time it wants to untangle. Dmitri Karamazov's pride and irascibility are as free as Aliosha's profound peace. The nature that stifles him and against which he struggles is not God-made but self-made; it is what he has sworn to be and what remains fixed because of the irreversibility of time. Alain says, in this connection, that a character is an oath. While reading M. Mauriac—and this may be to his credit—we dream of another Thérèse who might have been abler and greater. But it is the venerable antiquity and orthodoxy of this conflict between freedom and nature which finally commend it to us. It is the struggle of reason against the passions; the rebellion of the Christian soul, linked by the imagination to the body, against the body's appetites. Let us accept this theme provisionally, even though it may not seem true; it is enough that it be beautiful.

But is this "fatality" against which Thérèse must struggle merely the determinism of her inclinations? M. Mauriac calls it destiny. Let us not confuse destiny and character. Character is still ourselves; it is the combination of mild forces which insinuate themselves into our intentions and imperceptibly deflect our efforts, always in the same direction.

When Thérèse gets furious with Mondoux, who has humiliated her, M. Mauriac writes, "This time it was really she speaking, the Thérèse who was ready to tear things apart." Here it is really a question of Thérèse's character. But a little later, as she is leaving, after managing to make a wounding reply,[1] I read, "This sure-handed blow helped her to gauge her power, to become aware of her mission." What mission? Then I remember the following words from the preface: "the power given her to poison and corrupt". And there we have the destiny which envelops and prevails over the character and which represents, within Nature itself and in M. Mauriac's work, basely psychological as it sometimes is, the power of the Supernatural.

It is a fixed law, independent of Thérèse's will, that governs her acts as soon as they escape from her, and that leads them all, even the best-intentioned of them, to unhappy consequences. It reminds one of the fairy's punishment: "Every time you open your mouth, frogs will jump out." If you do not believe, this spell will have no meaning for you. But the believer understands it very well. What is it, after all, but the expression of that other spell, Original Sin? I therefore grant that M. Mauriac is in earnest when he speaks of destiny as a Christian. But when he speaks as a novelist, I can no longer follow him. Thérèse Desqueyroux's destiny is composed, on the one hand, of a flaw in her character and, on the other, of a curse that hangs over her acts. But these two factors are incompatible. One of them is visible from the inside, to the heroine herself; the other would require an infinite number of observations made from the outside by an observer intent on following Thérèse's acts to their ultimate consequences.

[1] I know of few scenes more vulgar than this one, and the curious thing is that this vulgarity must evidently be attributed to M. Mauriac himself.

M. Mauriac is so keenly aware of this that, when he wishes to show Thérèse as a predestined character, he resorts to an artifice; he shows her to us as she appears *to others*. "It was not surprising that people turned to look back as she passed; an evil-smelling animal betrays itself at once." Here, then, is the great hybrid presence we are made to see throughout the novel: Thérèse—though not limited to her pure freedom—Thérèse as she escapes from herself, to lose herself in a world of baleful fog. But how, then, can Thérèse know she has a destiny, if not because she already consents to it? And how does M. Mauriac know it? The idea of destiny is poetic and contemplative. But the novel is an action, and the novelist does not have the right to abandon the battlefield and settle himself comfortably on a hill as a spectator musing on The Fortunes of War.

But we must not think that M. Mauriac has accidentally surrendered for once to poetic temptation. This way of first identifying himself with his character and then abandoning her suddenly to consider her from the outside, like a judge, is characteristic of his art. He has, from the first, given us to understand that he was going to adopt Thérèse's point of view to tell the story, but, as a matter of fact, we immediately feel the translucent density of another consciousness between our eyes and Thérèse's room, her servant and the noises that rise from the street. But when, a few pages further on, we think we are still inside her, we have already left her; we are outside, with M. Mauriac, and we are looking at her.

The reason is that M. Mauriac makes use, for purposes of illusion, of the ambiguity of the "third person". In a novel, the pronoun "she" can designate *another*, that is, an opaque object, someone whose exterior is all we ever see—as when I write, for example, "I saw *that she* was trembling." But it also happens that this pronoun leads us into an intimacy which ought logically to express itself in the third person. "She was astounded to hear the echo of her own words." There is really no way of my knowing this unless I am in a position to say that I have heard the echo of my own words. In actual fact, novelists use this quite conventional mode of expression out of a kind of discretion, so as not to demand of the reader an unreserved complicity, so as to screen the dizzying intimacy of the *I*. The heroine's mind represents the opera-glass through which the reader can look into the fictional world, and the word "she" gives the illusion of the perspective of the opera-glass. It reminds us that this revealing consciousness is also a fictional creation; it represents a viewpoint on the privileged point of view and fulfills for the reader the fond desire of the lover to be both himself and someone else.

The same word has thus two opposing functions: "she-subject" and "she-object". M. Mauriac takes advantage of this indefiniteness in order to shift us imperceptibly from one aspect of Thérèse to another. "Thérèse was ashamed of her feelings." Very well. This Thérèse is a subject, that is, a *me*, kept at a certain distance from myself, and I experience this shame *inside Thérèse* because Thérèse herself knows that she feels it. But, in that case, since I read into her with her eyes, all I can ever know of her is what she knows—everything she knows, but nothing more.

In order to understand who Thérèse really *is*, I would have to break this complicity and close the book. All that would remain with me would be a memory of this consciousness, a consciousness still clear, but now hermetically closed, like all things of the past, and I would try to interpret it as though it were a fragment of my own earlier life. Now, at this point, while I am still in this absolute proximity with his characters, their dupe when they dupe themselves, their accomplice when they lie to themselves, M. Mauriac, suddenly and unbeknown to them, sends streaks of lightning through them, illuminating for me alone the essence of their beings, of which they are unaware and on which their characters have been struck as on a medal. "Never had the slightest relationship been established in Thérèse's mind between her unknown adventure and a criminal affair . . . *at least, in her conscious* mind", etc. . . . I find myself in a strange situation; I *am* Thérèse, and, at a certain aesthetic distance, she is myself. Her thoughts are my thoughts; as hers take shape, so do mine.

And yet I have insights into her which she does not have. Or else, seated in the centre of her consciousness, I help her lie to herself, and, at the same time, I judge and condemn her, I put myself inside her, as *another person*. "She could not help but be aware of her lie; she settled down into it, made her peace with it." This sentence gives a fair idea of the constant duplicity

M Mauriac requires of me. Thérèse lies to herself, reveals her lies and, nevertheless, tries to hide them from herself. This behaviour is something I have no way of knowing except through Thérèse herself. But the very way in which this attitude is revealed to me involves a pitiless judgment from without.

Besides, this uneasiness does not last long. Suddenly, by means of that "third person" whose ambiguity I have noted, M. Mauriac slips out, taking me along with him. " 'Make-up does wonders for you, my dear . . .' This was Thérèse's first remark, the remark of one woman to another." The flame of Thérèse's consciousness has gone out; this face, no longer lighted from within, has reassumed its compact opacity. But neither the name nor the pronoun which designates her, nor even the character of the narrative, has changed.

M. Mauriac finds this see-sawing so natural that he moves from Thérèse-subject to Thérèse-object within a single sentence. "She heard the clock strike nine. She had some time to kill, because it was still too early to take the pill which would assure her of a few hours' sleep; *not that such was the habit of this cautious and desperate woman,* but tonight she could not do without this aid." Who is judging Thérèse to be a "cautious and desperate woman"? It cannot be Thérèse herself. No, it is M. Mauriac, it is myself; we have the Desqueyroux record before us and we are pronouncing judgment.

But M. Mauriac plays other tricks as well. Like Asmodeus, that nosey and mischievous devil so dear to his heart, he likes to pry off the corners of roofs. When it suits his purpose, he leaves Thérèse and suddenly installs himself inside another character, whether it be Georges or Marie or Bernard Desqueyroux, or Anne the servant. He takes a look about and then trundles off, like a marionette. "Thérèse was unable to understand the meaning of that troubled look on the girl's face and *did not know* that the other was thinking, 'In all my life, I'll never live through half of what that old woman has been through in a few days.' " Didn't she know? It doesn't matter. M. Mauriac suddenly abandons her, leaves her to her ignorance, drops in on Marie and brings back a little snapshot for us.

On the other hand, at times he generously permits one of his creatures to share in the novelist's divine lucidity. "She stretched out her arms to draw him to her, but he drew violently away, and she *realized* that she had lost him." The indications are uncertain, and besides, they involve only the present. But what does it matter? M. Mauriac has decided that Georges is lost to Thérèse. He has decided, just as the ancient Gods decreed Oedipus' parricide and incest. Then, in order to inform us of his decree, he lends his creature, for a few moments, some of Tiresias' power of divination; have no fear; she will soon relapse into darkness. Besides, here is the curfew. The minds of all the characters go out. Tired, M. Mauriac suddenly withdraws from all of them. There remains only the façade of a world, a few puppets in a cardboard set:

The child spread the fingers that covered her eyes.
"I thought you were sleeping."
The voice begged her again, "Swear to me that you're happy."

There are gestures and sounds in the shadows. M. Mauriac is seated nearby, thinking, "'How you must have suffered, Mummy!' 'Oh no, I didn't feel a thing . . .' What? Could it be that the rattling in her throat and her purple face had not been signs of suffering? Can a person go through a hell of pain and then forget about it completely?"

It is obvious to anyone familiar with Marie's character that the girl wastes no time in such reflections. No, what we have here is rather M. Mauriac resting from his labours on the seventh day and thrilled with his creation.

And now here is the real reason for his failure. He once wrote that the novelist is to his own creatures what God is to His. And that explains all the oddities of his technique. He takes God's standpoint on his characters. God sees the inside and outside, the depths of body and soul, the whole universe at once. In like manner, M. Mauriac is omniscient about everything relating to his little world. What he says about his characters is Gospel. He explains them, categorizes them and condemns them without appeal. If anyone were to ask him how he knows that Thérèse is a cautious and desperate woman he would probably reply, with great surprise, "Didn't I create her?"

No, he didn't! The time has come to say that the novelist is not God. We would do well to recall the caution with which

Conrad suggests to us that Lord Jim may be "romantic". He takes great care not to state this himself; he puts the word into the mouth of one of his characters, a fallible being, who utters it hesitantly. The word "romantic", clear as it is, thereby acquires depth and pathos and a certain indefinable mystery. Not so with M. Mauriac. "A cautious and desperate woman" is no hypothesis; it is an illumination which comes to us from above. The author, impatient to have us grasp the character of his heroine, suddenly gives us the key. But what I maintain is precisely the fact that he has no right to make these absolute judgments. A novel is an action related from various points of view. And M. Mauriac is well aware of this, having written, in *La Fin de la Nuit*, that ". . . the most conflicting judgments about a single person can be correct; it is a question of lighting, and no one light reveals more than another". But each of these interpretations must be in motion, drawn along, so to speak, by the very action it interprets.

It is, in short, the testimony of a participant and should reveal the man who testifies as well as the event to which he testifies. It should arouse our impatience (will it be confirmed or denied by events?), and thus give us a feeling of the dragging of time. Thus, each point of view is relative, and the best one will be that which makes the reader feel most acutely the dragging of time. The participants' interpretations and explanations will all be hypothetical. The reader may have an inkling, beyond these conjectures, of the event's absolute reality, but it is for him alone to re-establish it. Should he care to try this sort of exercise, he will never get beyond the realm of likelihood and probability.

In any case, the introduction of absolute truth or of God's standpoint constitutes a twofold error of technique. To begin with, it presupposes a purely contemplative narrator, withdrawn from the action. This inevitably conflicts with Valéry's law of aesthetics, according to which any given element of a work of art ought always to maintain a plurality of relationships with the other elements. And besides, the absolute is nontemporal. If you pitch the narrative in the absolute, the string of duration snaps, and the novel disappears before your eyes. All that remains is a dull truth, *sub specie aeternitatis*.

But there is something even more serious. The definitive

judgments with which M. Mauriac is always ready to intersperse
the narrative prove that he does not conceive his characters
as he ought. He fabricates their natures before setting them
down, he decrees that they *will be* this or that. The essence of
Thérèse, the evil-smelling animal, the desperate and cautious
woman, is, I admit, complex, and not to be expressed in a
single sentence. But what exactly is this essence? Her inmost
depths? Let us look at it more closely. Conrad saw clearly that
the word "romantic" had meaning when it expressed an aspect
of character *for other people*. Such words as "desperate and
cautious" and "evil-smelling animal" and "castaway" and
other such neat phrases are of the same sort as the word that
Conrad puts into the mouth of the merchant of the islands.
When Thérèse resumes her story,

For years she had been unaware that the pattern of her destiny
had been a series of attempts to get out of a rut, each ending in
failure. But now that she had emerged from the darkness, she saw
clearly . . .

she is able to judge her past so easily only because she cannot
return to it. Thus, when he thinks he is probing the hearts of
his characters, M. Mauriac remains outside, at the door.

This would be quite all right if M. Mauriac were aware of it
and wrote novels like Hemingway's, in which we hardly know
the heroes except through their gestures and words, and the
vague judgments they pass on each other. But when M.
Mauriac, making full use of his creative authority, forces us to
accept these exterior views as the inner stuff of his creatures,
he is transforming his characters into *things*. Only things can
simply *be*; they have only exteriors. Minds cannot simply be;
they become. Thus, in shaping his Thérèse *sub specie aeternitatis*,
M. Mauriac first makes of her a thing, after which he adds, on
the sly, a whole mental thickness. But in vain. Fictional beings
have their laws, the most rigorous of which is the following:
the novelist may be either their witness or their accomplice,
but never both at the same time. The novelist must be either
inside or out. Because M. Mauriac does not observe these laws,
he does away with his characters' minds.

We are now back at freedom, Thérèse's other dimension.
What becomes of her in this darkened world? Until now,

Thérèse has been a *thing*, an ordered succession of motives and patterns, of passions, habits and interests, a *story* one could sum up in a few maxims—a *fatality*. This witch, this possessed creature, is now presented to us as free. M. Mauriac takes pains to tell us what we are to understand by this freedom.

But yesterday, in particular, when I decided to give up my fortune, I felt deep delight. I floated a thousand cubits *above my real self*. I climb, climb, climb . . . and then suddenly I slide back and find myself in that evil, cold, wilfulness, which is what I am when I make no effort, *which is what I fall back on when I fall back on myself*.[1]

Thus, freedom is not Thérèse's "real self" any more than consciousness is. This self, "what I fall back on when I fall back on myself", is a piece of data, a *thing*. Consciousness and freedom come later, consciousness as power to have illusions about oneself, and freedom as power to escape from oneself.

We must understand that for M. Mauriac, freedom cannot *construct*. A man, using his freedom, cannot create himself or forge his own history. Free will is merely a discontinuous force which allows for brief escapes, but which produces nothing, except a few short-lived events. Thus, *La Fin de la Nuit*, which, according to M. Mauriac, is the novel of someone's freedom, appears to be, above all, the story of an enslavement. So much so that the author, who, at first, wanted to show us "the stages of a spiritual ascension", confesses in his preface that Thérèse has led him, in spite of himself, into hell. "The finished work," he observes, not without regret, "disappoints in part the hopes contained in the title." But how could it have been otherwise?

Freedom, by the very fact of its having been thus tacked on to Thérèse's dense and fixed nature, loses its omnipotence and indeterminacy. Freedom itself is defined and characterized, since we know *in opposition to what* it is freedom. M. Mauriac goes even further and imposes a law upon it. "I climb, climb, climb . . . and then suddenly I slide back . . ." Thus, it is decreed in advance that Thérèse will sink back again each time. We are even informed in the preface that it would be indiscreet to ask more of her. "She belongs to that race of beings who emerge from darkness only when they depart from life. All that is asked

[1] The italics are mine.

of them is that they not resign themselves to darkness." It is Thérèse herself who speaks of the "pattern of her destiny". Freedom is a phase of this pattern. Even in her freedom, Thérèse is predictable. M. Mauriac has measured out with the precision of a doctor's prescription or of a cooking recipe the little freedom he allows her. I expect nothing from her: I know everything. Her ups and downs affect me little more than those of a cockroach climbing a wall with stupid obstinacy.

The reason is that no allowance has been made for freedom. Because Thérèse's freedom has been doled out with a dropper, it no more resembles real freedom than her mind resembles a real mind. And when M. Mauriac, absorbed in describing Thérèse's psychological mechanisms, wants us to feel that she is no longer a mechanism, he suddenly finds that he lacks the necessary devices. Of course he shows us Thérèse struggling against her evil inclinations. "Thérèse tightened her jaw. 'I won't talk about Garcin to him,' she said to herself." But what proof have I that a closer analysis would not reveal the deterministic links and reasons behind this sudden revolt? M. Mauriac feels this so acutely that occasionally, in desperation, he tugs at our sleeve and whispers, "Look! This time it's the real thing! She's free!" As in the following passage: "She interrupted herself in the middle of a sentence (for she was being entirely honest)." I know of no clumsier device than this parenthetical admonition, but the author is obviously obliged to use it.

On the basis of this hybrid creature of M. Mauriac's begetting which he calls Thérèse's nature, *there is no way of distinguishing between a free action and a passion*. But perhaps there is: through a sort of evanescent grace that plays over the features or the soul of a character fresh from a victory over himself:

The expression on her face was as beautiful as he had ever seen it.

She did not feel herself suffering, she felt relieved, delivered of some nameless burden, as if she were no longer going round in circles, as if she were suddenly going forward.

But these moral recompenses are not enough to convince us. On the contrary, they show us that, for M. Mauriac, freedom differs from slavery in *value*, and not in nature. Any intention directed upwards, toward Good, is free, and any will to Evil is fettered. It is needless for us to discuss the intrinsic worth of this distinguishing principle. In any case, it stifles freedom in fiction and, with it, the immediate duration which is the substance of the novel.

How *could* Thérèse's story have duration? It involves the old theological conflict between divine omniscience and human freedom. Thérèse's "pattern of destiny", the graph of her ups and downs, resembles a fever curve; it is dead time, since the future is spread out like the past and simply repeats it. The reader of a novel does not want to be God. In order for my duration to be transfused into the veins of Thérèse and Marie Desqueyroux, I must, at least once, be unaware of their fate and impatient to know it. But M. Mauriac does not bother to play upon my impatience. His sole aim is to make me as knowing as himself. He showers me with information. No sooner do I feel my curiosity begin to stir than it is satisfied beyond measure. Dostoevsky would have surrounded Thérèse with dense and mysterious figures whose meaning would have been at the brink of surrender on every page, only to elude my grasp. But M. Mauriac places me straight away in the very depths of his characters' hearts. No one has any secrets; he spreads an even light over everyone.

Thus, even if I were ever curious about the development of events, I could not identify my own impatience with that of Thérèse, since we are not waiting for the same things and what she would like to know, I have known for a long time. To me, she is like one of those abstract partners in the explanation of a bridge game who are kept in hypothetical ignorance of the opposing hands and who plan in terms of that very ignorance, whereas I can see all the cards already and know the errors in their hopes and calculations.

It is plain to see, moreover, that M. Mauriac has no liking for time, no fondness for the Bergsonian necessity of waiting "for the sugar to melt". To him, his creature's time is a dream, an all-too-human illusion; he gets rid of it and resolutely sets himself up within the eternal. But this alone, to my way of thinking, should have deterred him from writing novels. The real novelist is stirred by things that offer resistance; he is excited by doors because they must be opened, by envelopes because they must be unsealed.

In Hemingway's admirable *A Farewell to Arms*, objects are time-traps; they fill the narrative with innumerable tiny, obstinate resistances which the hero must break down one after the other. But M. Mauriac detests these lowly barriers that deter him from his purpose; he speaks of them as little as possible. He even wants to economize on the time of his characters' conversations; he suddenly speaks up for them and summarizes, in a few words, what they are going to say.

'Love,' said Thérèse, 'isn't everything in life—especially for men . . .' She went off on this theme. She could have talked till dawn; the sensible remarks she was making out of duty and with an effort were not the kind . . . etc.

There is, perhaps, no graver error in all the book than this stinginess. By cutting short the dialogue of his characters just when they begin to interest me, M. Mauriac projects me suddenly (and how can he fail to see this?) out of their time and out of their story. For these dialogues do not stop; I know they go on somewhere, but my right to sit in on them has been withdrawn. He would probably regard these sudden stops and sudden beginnings as "foreshortenings". I, for my part, prefer to regard them as breakdowns. Of course a novelist has to "foreshorten" now and then, but that does not in the least mean that he suddenly drains off the duration. In a novel, you must tell all or keep quiet; above all, you must not omit or skip anything. A foreshortening is simply a change of speed in the narration. M. Mauriac is in a hurry; he has probably sworn that no work of his will ever exceed the dimensions of a long short story.

I look in vain through *La Fin de la Nuit* for the long, stammering conversations, so frequent in English novels, in which the heroes are forever going over their stories, without managing to make them advance. I look in vain for the respites that suspend the action only to increase its urgency, the "between-times" in which, beneath a dark and cloudy sky, the characters busily absorb themselves in their familiar occupations. M. Mauriac treats only the essential passages, which he then joins together with brief summaries.

It is because of this taste for concision that his creatures talk as though they were in the theatre. M. Mauriac is interested only in getting them to say what they have to say as quickly and clearly as possible. Rejecting the superfluity, repetition and fumbling of actual speech, he gives to his heroes' remarks their naked power of significance. And since we must, nevertheless, be able to sense a difference between what he himself writes and what he makes them say, he imparts to these over-clear speeches a sort of torrential speed which is that of the theatre. Listen, for example, to Thérèse:

'What? How dare you? Do you mean to say I didn't commit the act? But I did. Though it is nothing compared to my other more cowardly, more secret crimes—crimes that involved no risk.'

This passage should be spoken aloud rather than read. Notice the oratorical movement of the beginning, and the question which swells with repetition. Doesn't it recall Hermione's jealous rages in *Andromaque*? I catch myself whispering the words aloud, struck by that rhetorical beginning typical of all good tragic dialogue. Now read this:

'However rash your friend may be, he cannot be so rash as to think you attractive. Had I meant to make him jealous, I should have taken more care to make the matter seem credible.'

Doesn't the reader recognize the turn of phrase dear to the comic writers of the eighteenth century? The novel is not at all suited to graces of this kind, not because people ought to talk in the novel as they do in life, but because the novel has its own kind of stylization. The transition to dialogue ought to be marked by a kind of flickering of the lights. It is dark, the hero struggles to express himself; his words are not pictures of his soul, but rather free and clumsy acts, which say too much and too little. The reader gets impatient; he tries to see beyond these involved and fumbling statements. Dostoevsky, Conrad and Faulkner have known how to use this resistance of words, which is a source of endless misunderstandings and involuntary revelations, and thereby to make of dialogue "the fictional moment", the time when the sense of duration is richest. M.

Mauriac's classicism is probably repelled by such woolly conversation. But everyone knows that French classicism is rhetorical and theatrical.

Nor is this all. M. Mauriac also insists that each of these conversations be effective and, consequently, he complies with another theatrical law—for it is only in the theatre that the dialogue must keep the action going forward. He therefore builds up "scenes". The entire novel is made up of four scenes each of which ends in a "catastrophe". Each scene is prepared exactly as in a tragedy.

Take, for example, the following: At Saint-Clair, Marie receives a letter from Georges, her fiancé, who backs out of his engagement. Convinced, through a misunderstanding, that her mother is responsible for the break, she leaves immediately for Paris. We know all about this turbulent, selfish, passionate, rather silly girl, who is also capable of good impulses. She is shown during this journey as being mad with rage, her claws bared, determined to fight, to wound, to pay back with interest the blows she has received. Thérèse's state is described with no less precision. We know that she has been consumed by suffering, that she is half out of her mind. Is it not obvious that the meeting of these two women is brought about as in a play? We know the forces present. The situation is rigorously defined; it is a confrontation. Marie does not know that her mother is mad. What will she do when she realizes it? The problem is clearly formulated.

We have only to leave everything to determinism, with its movements and counter-movements, its dramatic and anticipated reversals. It will lead us inevitably to the final catastrophe, with Marie playing the nurse and prevailing upon her mother to come back to the Desqueyroux home. Doesn't this recall Sardou or the great scene in Bernstein's *The Spy*, or the second act of *The Thief*? I quite understand M. Mauriac's being tempted by the theatre. While reading *La Fin de la Nuit*, I felt, time and again, as if I were reading the argument and chief passages of a four-act play.

Let us look at the passage in *Beauchamp's Career* where Meredith shows us the last meeting of Beauchamp and Renée. They are still in love and are within an ace of confessing their feelings, but they part. When they meet, *anything* is possible between them. The future does not yet exist. Gradually their little weaknesses and mistakes and resentments begin to get the better of their good will. They cease to see straight. Nevertheless, up to the very end, even when I begin to fear that they may break up, I still feel that *it may all still work out*. The reason is that they are free. Their final separation will be of their own making. *Beauchamp's Career* is a novel!

La Fin de la Nuit is not a novel. How can anyone call this angular, glacial book, with its analyses, theatrical passages and poetic meditations, a "novel"? How can anyone confuse these bursts of speed and violent jamming of the brakes, these abrupt starts and breakdowns, with the majestic flow of fictional time? How can anyone be taken in by this motionless narrative, which betrays its intellectual framework from the very start, in which the mute faces of the heroes are inscribed like angles in a circle? If it is true that a novel is a *thing*, like a painting or architectural structure, if it is true that a novel is made with time and free minds, as a picture is painted with oil and pigments, then *La Fin de la Nuit* is not a novel. It is, at most, a collection of signs and intentions. M. Mauriac is not a novelist.

Why? Why hasn't this serious and earnest writer achieved his purpose? Because, I think, of the sin of pride. Like most of our writers, he has tried to ignore the fact that the theory of relativity applies in full to the universe of fiction, that there is no more place for a privileged observer in a real novel than in the world of Einstein, and that it is no more possible to conduct an experiment in a fictional system[1] in order to determine whether the system is in motion or at rest than there is in a physical system. M. Mauriac has put himself first. He has chosen divine omniscience and omnipotence. But novels are written *by* men and *for* men. In the eyes of God, Who cuts through appearances and goes beyond them, there is no novel, no art, for art thrives on appearances. God is not an artist. Neither is M. Mauriac.

(*February* 1939.)

---

[1] By fictional system, I mean the novel as a whole, as well as the partial systems that make it up (the minds of the characters, their combined psychological and moral judgments).

II

Camus' "The Outsider"

M. CAMUS' *The Outsider* was barely off the press when it began to arouse the widest interest. People told each other that it was "the best book since the end of the war". Amidst the literary productions of its time, this novel was, itself, an outsider. It came to us from the other side of the Equator, from across the sea. In that bitter spring of the coal shortage, it spoke to us of the sun, not as of an exotic marvel, but with the weary familiarity of those who have had too much of it. It was not concerned with re-burying the old regime with its own hands, nor with filling us with a sense of our own unworthiness.

We remembered, while reading this novel, that there had once been works which had not tried to prove anything, but had been content to stand on their own merits. But hand in hand with its gratuitousness went a certain ambiguity. How were we to interpret this character who, the day after his mother's death, "went swimming, started a liaison with a girl and went to see a comic film", who killed an Arab "because of the sun", who claimed, on the eve of his execution, that he "had been happy and still was", and hoped there would be a lot of spectators at the scaffold "to welcome him with cries of hate". "He's a poor fool, an idiot", some people said; others, with greater insight, said, "He's innocent." The meaning of this innocence still remained to be understood.

In *The Myth of Sisyphus*, which appeared a few months later, M. Camus provided us with a precise commentary upon his work. His hero was neither good nor bad, neither moral nor immoral. These categories do not apply to him. He belongs to a very particular species for which the author reserves the word "absurd". But in M. Camus' work this word takes on two very different meanings. The absurd is both a state of fact and the lucid awareness which certain people acquire of this state of fact. The "absurd" man is the man who does not hesitate to draw the inevitable conclusions from a fundamental absurdity.

There is the same displacement of meaning as when we give the name "swing" to the youthful generation that dances to "swing" music. What is meant by the absurd as a state of fact, as primary situation? It means nothing less than man's relation to the world. Primary absurdity manifests a cleavage, the cleavage between man's aspirations to unity and the insurmountable dualism of mind and nature, between man's drive toward the eternal and the *finite* character of his existence, between the "concern" which constitutes his very essence and the vanity of his efforts. Chance, death, the irreducible pluralism of life and of truth, the unintelligibility of the real—all these are extremes of the absurd.

These are not really very new themes, and M. Camus does not present them as such. They had been sounded as early as the seventeenth century by a certain kind of dry, plain, contemplative rationalism, which is typically French and they served as the commonplaces of classical pessimism.

Was it not Pascal who emphasized "the natural misfortune of our mortal and feeble condition, so wretched that when we consider it closely, nothing can console us"? Was it not he who put reason in its place? Would he not have wholeheartedly approved the following remark of M. Camus: "The world is neither (completely) rational, nor quite irrational either"? Does he not show us that "custom" and "diversion" conceal man's "nothingness, his forlornness, his inadequacy, his impotence and his emptiness" from himself? By virtue of the cool style of *The Myth of Sisyphus* and the subject of his essays, M. Camus takes his place in the great tradition of those French moralists whom Andler has rightly termed the precursors of Nietzsche.

As to the doubts raised by M. Camus about the scope of our reasoning powers, these are in the most recent tradition of French epistemology. If we think of scientific nominalism, of Poincaré, Duhem and Meyerson, we are better able to understand the reproach our author addresses to modern science. "You tell me of an invisible planetary system in which electrons revolve about a nucleus. You explain the world to me by means of an image. I then realize that you have ended in poetry . . ."[1] This idea was likewise expressed, and at just about the same time, by another writer, who draws on the same material when he says, "Physics uses mechanical, dynamic and even psychological models without any preference, as if, freed of ontological aspirations, it were becoming indifferent to the classical antimonies of the mechanism or dynamism which presupposes a nature-in-itself."[2] M. Camus shows off a bit by quoting passages from Jaspers, Heidegger and Kierkegaard, whom, by the way, he does not always seem to have quite understood. But his real masters are to be found elsewhere.

The turn of his reasoning, the clarity of his ideas, the cut of his expository style and a certain kind of solar, ceremonious and sad sombreness, all indicate a classic temperament, a man of the Mediterranean. His very method ("only through a balance of evidence and lyricism shall we attain a combination of emotion and lucidity.")[3] recalls the old "passionate geometries" of Pascal and Rousseau and relate him, for example, not to a German phenomenologist or a Danish existentialist, but rather to Maurras, that other Mediterranean from whom, however, he differs in many respects.

But M. Camus would probably be willing to grant all this. To him, originality means pursuing one's ideas to the limit; it certainly does not mean making a collection of pessimistic maxims. The absurd, to be sure, resides neither in man nor in the world, if you consider each separately. But since man's dominant characteristic is "being-in-the-world", the absurd is, in the end, an inseparable part of the human condition. Thus, the absurd is not, to begin with, *the object of a mere idea; it is revealed to us in a doleful illumination.* "Getting up, tram, four hours of work, meal, sleep, and Monday, Tuesday, Wednesday, Thursday, Friday, Saturday, in the same routine . . .",[4] and then, suddenly, "the setting collapses", and we find ourselves in a state of hopeless lucidity.

If we are able to refuse the misleading aid of religion or of existential philosophies, we then possess certain basic, obvious facts: the world is chaos, a "divine equivalence born of

[1] *The Myth of Sisyphus.*
[2] M. Merleau Ponty, *La Structure du Comportement.*
[3] *The Myth of Sisyphus.*
[4] *Ibid.*

anarchy"; tomorrow does not exist, since we all die. "In a universe suddenly deprived of light and illusions, man feels himself an outsider. This exile is irrevocable, since he has no memories of a lost homeland and no hope of a promised land."[1] The reason is that man *is not* the world. "If I were a tree among other trees . . . this life would have a meaning, or rather this problem would have none, for I would be part of this world. I *would be* this world against which I set myself with my entire mind . . . It is preposterous reason which sets me against all creation."[2] This explains, in part, the title of our novel; the outsider is man confronting the world. M. Camus might as well have chosen the title of one of George Gissing's works, *Born in Exile*. The outsider is also man among men. "There are days when . . . you find that the person you've loved has become a stranger."[3] The stranger is, finally, myself in relation to myself, that is, natural man in relation to mind: "The stranger who, at certain moments, confronts us in a mirror."[4]

But that is not all; there is a *passion* of the absurd. The absurd man will not commit suicide; he wants to live, without relinquishing any of his certainty, without a future, without hope, without illusion and without resignation either. He stares at death with passionate attention and this fascination liberates him. He experiences the "divine irresponsibility" of the condemned man.

Since God does not exist and man dies, everything is permissible. One experience is as good as another; the important thing is simply to acquire as many as possible. "The ideal of the absurd man is the present and the succession of present moments before an ever-conscious spirit."[5] Confronted with this "quantitative ethic" all values collapse; thrown into this world, the absurd man, rebellious and irresponsible, has "nothing to justify". He is *innocent*, innocent as Somerset Maugham's savages before the arrival of the clergyman who teaches them Good and Evil, what is lawful and what is forbidden. For this man, *everything* is lawful. He is as innocent as Prince Mishkin, who "lives in an everlasting present, lightly

[1] *The Myth of Sisyphus.*
[2] *Ibid.*
[3] *Ibid.*
[4] *Ibid.*
[5] *Ibid.*

tinged with smiles and indifference." Innocent in every sense of the word, he too is, if you like, an "Idiot".

And now we fully understand the title of Camus' novel. The outsider he wants to portray is precisely one of those terrible innocents who shock society by not accepting the rules of its game. He lives among outsiders, but to them, too, he is an outsider. That is why some people like him—for example, his mistress, Marie, who is fond of him "because he's odd". Others, like the courtroom crowd whose hatred he suddenly feels mounting towards him, hate him for the same reason. And we ourselves, who, on opening the book are not yet familiar with the feeling of the absurd, vainly try to judge him according to our usual standards. For us, too, he is an outsider.

Thus, the shock you felt when you opened the book and read, "I thought that here was another Sunday over with, that Mama was buried now, that I would go back to work again and that, on the whole, nothing had changed," was deliberate. It was the result of your first encounter with the absurd. But you probably hoped that as you progressed your uneasiness would fade, that everything would be slowly clarified, would be given a reasonable justification and explained. Your hopes were disappointed. *The Outsider* is not an explanatory book. The absurd man does not explain; he describes. Nor is it a book which proves anything.

M. Camus is simply presenting something and is not concerned with a justification of what is fundamentally unjustifiable. *The Myth of Sisyphus* teaches us how to accept our author's novel. In it, we find the theory of the novel of absurdity. Although the absurdity of the human condition is its sole theme, it is not a novel with a message; it does not come out of a "satisfied" kind of thinking, intent on furnishing formal proofs. It is rather the product of a thinking which is "limited, rebellious and mortal". It is a proof in itself of the futility of abstract reasoning. "The fact that certain great novelists have chosen to write in terms of images rather than of arguments reveals a great deal about a certain kind of thinking common to them all, a conviction of the futility of all explanatory principles, and of the instructive message of sensory impressions."[1]

[1] *The Myth of Sisyphus.*

Thus, the very fact that M. Camus delivers his message in the form of a novel reveals a proud humility. This is not resignation, but the rebellious recognition of the limitations of human thought. It is true that he felt obliged to make a philosophical translation of his fictional message. *The Myth of Sisyphus* is just that, and we shall see later on how we are to interpret this parallel commentary. But the existence of the translation does not, in any case, alter the gratuitousness of the novel.

The man who creates in absurdity has lost even the illusion of his work's necessity. He wants us, on the contrary, to be constantly aware of its contingent nature. He would like to see, inscribed below it, "might never have been", as Gide wanted "could be continued" written at the end of *The Coiners*. This novel might not have been, like some stone or stream or face. It is a thing in the present that happens, quite simply, like all other happenings in the present. It has not even the subjective necessity that artists pretend to when, speaking of their works, they say, "I had to write it, I had to get it off my chest." In it we find one of the themes of surrealist terrorism sifted through the classic sun. The work of art is only a leaf torn from a life. It does, of course, express this life. But it need not express it. And besides, everything has the same value, whether it be writing *The Possessed* or drinking a cup of coffee.

M. Camus does not require that attentive solicitude that writers who "have sacrificed their lives to art" demand of the reader. *The Outsider* is a leaf from his life. And since the most absurd life is that which is most sterile, his novel aims at being magnificently sterile. Art is an act of unnecessary generosity. We need not be over-disturbed by this; I find, hidden beneath M. Camus' paradoxes, some of Kant's wise observations on the "endless end" of the beautiful. Such, in any case, is *The Outsider*, a work detached from a life, unjustified and unjustifiable, sterile, momentary, already forsaken by its author, abandoned for other present things. And that is how we must accept it, as a brief communion between two men, the author and the reader, beyond reason, in the realm of the absurd.

This will give us some idea as to how we are to regard the hero of *The Outsider*. If M. Camus had wanted to write a novel with a purpose, he would have had no difficulty in showing a civil servant lording it over his family, and then suddenly struck with the intuition of the absurd, struggling against it for a while and finally resolving to live out the fundamental absurdity of his condition. The reader would have been convinced along with the character, and for the same reasons.

Or else, he might have related the life of one of those saints of the Absurd, so dear to his heart, of whom he speaks in *The Myth of Sisyphus*: Don Juan, the Actor, the Conqueror, the Creator. But he has not done so, and Meursault, the hero of *The Outsider*, remains ambiguous, even to the reader who is familiar with theories of the absurd. We are, of course, assured that he is absurd, and his dominant characteristic is a pitiless clarity. Besides, he is, in more ways than one, constructed so as to furnish a concerted illustration of the theories expounded in *The Myth of Sisyphus*. For example, in the latter work, M. Camus writes, "A man's virility lies more in what he keeps to himself than in what he says." And Meursault is an example of this virile silence, of this refusal to indulge in words: "[He was asked] if he had noticed that I was withdrawn, and he admitted only that I didn't waste words."[1] And two lines before this, the same witness has just declared that Meursault "was a man". "[He was asked] what he meant by that, and he said that everyone knew what he meant."

In like manner M. Camus expatiates on love in *The Myth of Sisyphus*. "It is only on the basis of a collective way of seeing, for which books and legends are responsible, that we give the name *love* to what binds us to certain human beings."[2] And similarly, we read in *The Outsider*: "So she wanted to know whether I loved her. I answered . . . that it didn't mean anything, but that I probably didn't love her."[3] From this point of view, the debate in the courtroom and in the reader's mind as to whether or not Meursault loved his mother is doubly absurd.

First of all, as the lawyer asks, "Is he accused of having buried his mother or of having killed a man?" But above all, the words "to love" are meaningless. Meursault probably put

[1] *The Outsider.*
[2] *The Myth of Sisyphus.*
[3] *The Outsider.*

his mother into an old people's home because he hadn't enough money and because "they had nothing more to say to one another". And he probably did not go to see her often, "because it wasted [his] Sunday—not to speak of the effort involved in getting to the bus, buying tickets and taking a two-hour trip."[1] But what does this mean? Isn't he living completely in the present, according to his present fancies? What we call a feeling is merely the abstract unity and the meaning of discontinuous impressions.

I am not constantly thinking about the people I love, but I claim to love them even when I am not thinking about them —and I am capable of compromising my well-being in the name of an abstract feeling, in the absence of any real and immediate emotion. Meursault thinks and acts in a different way; he has no desire to know these noble, continuous, completely identical feelings. For him, neither love nor individual loves exist. All that counts is the present and the concrete. He goes to see his mother when he feels like it, and that's that.

If the desire is there, it will be strong enough to make this sluggard run at full speed to jump into a moving truck. But he still calls his mother by the tender, childish name of "Mama", and he never misses a chance to understand her and identify himself with her. "All I know of love is that mixture of desire, tenderness and intelligence that binds me to someone."[2] Thus we see that the *theoretical* side of Meursault's character is not to be overlooked. In the same way, many of his adventures are intended chiefly to bring out some aspect or other of the basic absurdity of things. *The Myth of Sisyphus*, for example, extols, as we have seen, the "perfect freedom of the condemned prisoner to whom, some particular daybreak, the prison doors swing open"[3], and it is in order to make us taste this daybreak and freedom that M. Camus has condemned his hero to capital punishment. "How could I have failed to see," says Meursault, "that nothing was more important than an execution . . . and that it was even, in a way, the only really interesting thing for a man!" One could multiply the examples and quotations.

[1] *The Outsider.*
[2] *The Myth of Sisyphus.*
[3] *Ibid.*

Nevertheless, this lucid, indifferent, taciturn man is not entirely constructed to serve a cause. Once the character had been sketched in, he probably completed himself; he certainly had a real weight of his own. Still, his absurdity seems to have been given rather than achieved; that's how he is, and that's that. He does have his revelation on the last page, but he has always lived according to M. Camus' standards. If there were a grace of absurdity, we would have to say that he has grace. He does not seem to pose himself any of the questions explored in *The Myth of Sisyphus*; Meursault is not shown rebelling at his death sentence. He was happy, he has let himself live, and his happiness does not seem to have been marred by that hidden gnawing which M. Camus frequently mentions in his essay and which is due to the blinding presence of death. His very indifference often seems like indolence, as, for instance, that Sunday when he stays at home out of pure laziness, and when he admits to having been "slightly bored". The character thus retains a real opacity, even to the absurd-conscious observer. He is no Don Juan, no Don Quixote of the absurd; he often even seems like its Sancho Panza. He is there before us, he exists, and we can neither understand nor quite judge him. In a word, he is alive, and all that can justify him to us is his fictional density.

The Outsider is not, however, to be regarded as a completely gratuitous work. M. Camus distinguishes, as we have mentioned, between the *notion* and the *feeling* of the absurd. He says, in this connection, "Deep feelings, like great works, are always more meaningful than they are aware of being. . . . An intense feeling carries with it its own universe, magnificent or wretched, as the case may be."[1] And he adds, a bit further on, "The feeling of the absurd is not the same as the *idea* of the absurd. The idea is grounded in the feeling, that is all. It does not exhaust it." *The Myth of Sisyphus* might be said to aim at giving us this *idea*, and *The Outsider* at giving us the feeling.

The order in which the two works appeared seems to confirm this hypothesis. *The Outsider*, the first to appear, plunges us without comment into the "climate" of the absurd; the essay then comes and illumines the landscape. Now,

[1] *The Myth of Sisyphus*.

absurdity means divorce, discrepancy. *The Outsider* is to be a novel of discrepancy, divorce and disorientation; hence its skilful construction.

We have, on the one hand, the amorphous, everyday flow of reality as it is experienced, and, on the other, the edifying reconstruction of this reality by speech and human reason. The reader, brought face to face with simple reality, must find it again, without being able to recognize it in its rational transposition. This is the source of the feeling of the absurd, that is, of our inability to *think*, with our words and concepts, what happens in the world. Meursault buries his mother, takes a mistress and commits a crime.

These various facts will be related by witnesses at his trial, and they will be put in order and explained by the public prosecutor. Meursault will have the impression that they are talking of someone else. Everything is so arranged as to bring on the sudden outburst of Marie, who, after giving, in the witness-box, an account composed according to human rules, bursts into sobs and says "that that wasn't it, that there was something else, that they were forcing her to say the opposite of what she really thought". These mirror-tricks have been used frequently since *The Coiners*, and they do not constitute M. Camus' originality. But the problem to be solved imposes an original form upon him.

In order to feel the divergence between the prosecutor's conclusions and the actual circumstances of the murder, in order, when we have finished the book, to retain the impression of an absurd justice, incapable of ever understanding or even of making contact with the deeds it intends to punish, we must first have been placed in contact with reality, or with one of these circumstances. But in order to establish this contact, M. Camus, like the prosecutor, has only words and concepts at his disposal. In assembling thoughts, he is forced to use words to describe a world that precedes words. The first part of *The Outsider* could have been given the same title as a recent book, *Translated from Silence*. Here we touch upon a disease common to many contemporary writers and whose first traces I find in Jules Renard. I shall call it "the obsession with silence". M. Paulhan would certainly regard it as an effect of literary terrorism.

It has assumed a thousand forms, ranging from the sur-realists' automatic writing to Jean-Jacques Bernard's "theatre of silence". The reason is that silence, as Heidegger says, is the authentic mode of speech. Only the man who knows how to talk can be silent. M. Camus talks a great deal; in *The Myth of Sisyphus* he is even garrulous. And yet, he reveals his love of silence. He quotes Kierkegaard: "The surest way of being mute is not to hold your tongue, but to talk."[1] And he himself adds that "a man is more of a man because of what he does not say than what he does say". Thus, in *The Outsider*, he has attempted *to be silent*. But how is one to be silent with words? How is one to convey through concepts the unthinkable and disorderly succession of present instants? This problem involves resorting to a new technique.

What is this new technique? "It's Kafka written by Hemingway," I was told. I confess that I have found no trace of Kafka in it. M. Camus' views are entirely of this earth, and Kafka is the novelist of impossible transcendence; for him, the universe is full of signs that we cannot understand; there is a reverse side to the décor. For M. Camus, on the contrary, the tragedy of human existence lies in the absence of any transcendence. "I do not know whether this world has a mean-ing that is beyond me. But I do know that I am unaware of this meaning and that, for the time being, it is impossible for me to know it. What can a meaning beyond my condition mean to me? I can understand only in human terms. I understand the things I touch, things that offer me resistance."

He is not concerned, then, with so ordering words as to suggest an inhuman, undecipherable order; the inhuman is merely the disorderly, the mechanical. There is nothing am-biguous in his work, nothing disquieting, nothing hinted at. *The Outsider* gives us a succession of luminously clear views. If they bewilder us, it is only because of their number and the absence of any link between them. M. Camus likes bright mornings, clear evenings and relentless afternoons. His favourite season is Algiers' eternal summer. Night has hardly any place in his universe.

When he does talk of it, it is in the following terms: "I

[1] Quoted in *The Myth of Sisyphus*. Note also Brice Parain's theory of language and his conception of silence.

awakened with stars about my face. Country noises reached my ears. My temples were soothed by odours of night, earth and salt. The wonderful peace of that sleepy summer invaded me like a tide."[1] The man who wrote these lines is as far removed as possible from the anguish of a Kafka. He is very much at peace within disorder. Nature's obstinate blindness probably irritates him, but it comforts him as well. Its irrationality is only a negative thing. The absurd man is a humanist; he knows only the good things of this world.

The comparison with Hemingway seems more fruitful. The relationship between the two styles is obvious. Both men write in the same short sentences. Each sentence refuses to exploit the momentum accumulated by preceding ones. Each is a new beginning. Each is like a snapshot of a gesture or object. For each new gesture and word there is a new and corresponding sentence. Nevertheless, I am not quite satisfied. The existence of an "American" narrative technique has certainly been of help to M. Camus. I doubt whether it has, strictly speaking, influenced him.

Even in *Death in the Afternoon*, which is not a novel, Hemingway retains that abrupt style of narration that shoots each separate sentence out of the void with a sort of respiratory spasm. His style is himself. We know that M. Camus has another style, a ceremonious one. But even in *The Outsider* he occasionally heightens the tone. His sentences then take on a larger, more continuous, movement. "The cry of the newsvendors in the relaxed air, the last birds in the square, the calls of the sandwich-vendors, the wail of the trams on the high curves of the city and the distant murmur in the sky before night began to teeter over the port, all set before me a blind man's route with which I was familiar long before entering prison."[2]

Through the transparency of Meursault's breathless account I catch a glimpse of a poetic prose underneath, which is probably M. Camus' personal mode of expression. If *The Outsider* exhibits such visible traces of the American technique, it was deliberate on M. Camus' part. He has chosen from among all the instruments at his disposal the one which seemed to

[1] *The Outsider.*
[2] *Ibid.*

serve his purpose best. I doubt whether he will use it again
in future works.

Let us examine the plot a little more closely; we shall get
a clearer notion of the author's methods. "Men also secrete
the inhuman," writes M. Camus. "Sometimes, in moments
of lucidity, the mechanical aspect of their gestures and their
senseless pantomime make everything about them seem
stupid."[1] This quality must be rendered at once. *The Outsider*
must put us right from the start "into a state of uneasiness
when confronted with man's inhumanity".

But what are the particular occasions that create this
uneasiness in us? *The Myth of Sisyphus* gives us an example.
"A man is talking on the telephone. We cannot hear him behind
the glass partition, but we can see his senseless mimicry. We
wonder why he is alive?"[2] This answers the question almost
too well, for the example reveals a certain bias in the author.
The gesturing of a man who is telephoning and whom we
cannot hear is really only *relatively* absurd, because it is part
of an incomplete circuit. Listen in on an extension, however,
and the circuit is completed; human activity recovers its
meaning. Therefore, one would have, in all honesty, to admit
that there are only relative absurdities and only in relation to
"absolute rationalities".

However, we are not concerned with honesty, but with art.
M. Camus has a method ready to hand. He is going to insert
a glass partition between the reader and his characters. Is
there really anything sillier than a man behind a glass window?
Glass seems to let everything through. It stops only one thing:
the meaning of his gestures. The glass remains to be chosen.
It will be the Outsider's mind, which is really transparent,
since we see everything it sees. However, it is so constructed as
to be transparent to things and opaque to meanings.

"From then on, everything went very quickly. The men
went up to the coffin with a sheet. The priest, his followers,
the director and I, all went outside. In front of the door was
a lady I didn't know. 'Monsieur Meursault,' said the director.
I didn't hear the lady's name, and I gathered only that she was
a nurse who'd been ordered to be present. Without smiling,

[1] *The Myth of Sisyphus.*
[2] *Ibid.*

she nodded her long, bony face. Then we stood aside to make room for the body to pass."[1]

Some men are dancing behind a glass partition. Between them and the reader has been interposed a consciousness, something very slight, a translucent curtain, a pure passivity that merely records all the facts. But it has done the trick. Just because it is passive, this consciousness records only facts. The reader has not noticed this presence. But what is the assumption implied by this kind of narrative technique? To put it briefly, what had once been melodic structure has been transformed into a sum of invariant elements. This succession of *movements* is supposed to be rigorously identical with the *act* considered as a complete entity. Are we not dealing here with the analytic assumption that any reality is reducible to a sum total of elements? Now, though analysis may be the instrument of science, it is also the instrument of humour. If in describing a rugby match, I write, "I saw adults in shorts fighting and throwing themselves on the ground in order to send a leather ball between a pair of wooden posts," I have summed up what I have *seen*, but I have intentionally missed its meaning. I am merely trying to be humorous. M. Camus' story is analytic and humorous. Like all artists, he *invents*, because he pretends to be reconstituting raw experience and because he slyly eliminates all the significant links which are also part of the experience.

That is what Hume did when he stated that he could find nothing in experience but isolated impressions. That is what the American neo-realists still do when they deny the existence of any but external relations between phenomena. Contemporary philosophy has, however, established the fact that meanings are also part of the immediate data. But this would carry us too far afield. We shall simply indicate that the universe of the absurd man is the analytic world of the neo-realists. In literature, this method has proved its worth. It was Voltaire's method in *L'Ingénu* and *Micromégas*, and Swift's in *Gulliver's Travels*. For the eighteenth century also had its own outsiders, "noble savages", usually, who, transported to a strange civilization, perceived facts before being able to grasp their meaning. The effect of this discrepancy was to arouse in

[1] *The Outsider*.

the reader the feeling of the absurd. M. Camus seems to have this in mind on several occasions, particularly when he shows his hero reflecting on the reasons for his imprisonment.

It is this analytic process that explains the use of the American technique in *The Outsider*. The presence of death at the end of our path has made our future go up in smoke; our life has "no future", it is a series of present moments. What does this mean, if not that the absurd man is applying his analytical spirit to Time? Where Bergson saw an indestructible organization, he sees only a series of instants. It is the plurality of incommunicable moments that will finally account for the plurality of beings. What our author borrows from Hemingway is thus the discontinuity between the clipped phrases that imitate the discontinuity of time.

We are now in a better position to understand the form of his narrative. Each sentence is a present instant, but not an indecisive one that spreads like a stain to the following one. The sentence is sharp, distinct and self-contained. It is separated by a void from the following one, just as Descartes' instant is separated from the one that follows it. The world is destroyed and reborn from sentence to sentence. When the word makes its appearance it is a creation *ex nihilo*. The sentences in *The Outsider* are islands. We bounce from sentence to sentence, from void to void. It was in order to emphasize the isolation of each sentence unit that M. Camus chose to tell his story in the present perfect tense.[1] The simple past is the tense of continuity: "*Il se promena longtemps.*" These words refer us to a past perfect, to a future. The reality of the sentence is the verb, the act, with its transitive character and its transcendence. "*Il s'est promené longtemps*" conceals the verbality of the verb. The verb is split and broken in two.

On the one hand, we find a past participle which has lost all transcendence and which is as inert as a thing; and on the other, we find only the verb "être", which has merely a copulative sense and which joins the participle to the substantive as the attribute to the subject. The transitive character of the

[1] The following passage dealing with M. Camus' use of tenses is not intelligible in translation. The simple past tense in French is almost never used in conversation; it is limited almost exclusively to written narration; the usual French equivalent of the English past is the present perfect. (Translator's note.)

verb has vanished; the sentence has frozen. Its present reality becomes the noun. Instead of acting as a bridge between past and future, it is merely a small, isolated, self-sufficient substance.

If, in addition, you are careful to reduce it as much as possible to the main proposition, its internal structure attains a perfect simplicity. It gains thereby in cohesiveness. It becomes truly indivisible, an atom of time. The sentences are not, of course, arranged in relation to each other; they are simply juxtaposed. In particular, all causal links are avoided lest they introduce the germ of an explanation and an order other than that of pure succession. Consider the following passage: "She asked me, a moment later, if I loved her. *I answered that it didn't mean anything, but that I probably didn't love her. She seemed sad.* But while preparing lunch, for no reason at all she suddenly laughed in such a way that I kissed her. Just then, the noise of an argument broke out at Raymond's place." I have cited two sentences which most carefully conceal the causal link under the simple appearance of succession.

When it is absolutely necessary to allude to a preceding sentence, the author uses words like "and", "but", "then" and "just then", which evoke only disjunction, opposition or mere addition. The relations between these temporal units, like those established between objects by the neo-realists, are external. Reality appears on the scene without being introduced and then disappears without being destroyed. The world dissolves and is reborn with each pulsation of time. But we must not think it is self-generated. Any activity on its part would lead to a substitution by dangerous forces for the reassuring disorder of pure chance.

A nineteenth-century naturalist would have written "A bridge spanned the river." M. Camus will have none of this anthropomorphism. He says "Over the river was a bridge." This object thus immediately betrays its passiveness. It *is there* before us, plain and undifferentiated. "There were four negro men in the room . . . in front of the door was a lady I didn't know. . . . Beside her was the director. . . ." People used to say that Jules Renard would end by writing things like "The hen lays." M. Camus and many other contemporary writers would write "There is the hen and she lays." The reason is that they like things for their own sake and do not want to dilute them in the flux of duration. "There is water." Here we have a bit of eternity—passive, impenetrable, incommunicable and gleaming! What sensual delight, if only we could touch it! To the absurd man, this is the one and only good. And that is why the novelist prefers these short-lived little sparkles, each of which gives a bit of pleasure, to an organized narrative.

This is what enables M. Camus to think that in writing *The Outsider* he remains silent. His sentence does not belong to the universe of discourse. It has neither ramifications nor extensions nor internal structure. It might be defined, like Valéry's sylph, as

> *Neither seen nor known:*
> *The time of a bare breast*
> *Between two shifts.*

It is very exactly measured by the time of a silent intuition. If this is so, can we speak of M. Camus' novel as something whole? All the sentences of his book are equal to each other, just as all the absurd man's experiences are equal. Each one sets up for itself and sweeps the others into the void. But, as a result, no single one of them detaches itself from the background of the others, except for the rare moments in which the author, abandoning these principles, becomes poetic.

The very dialogues are integrated into the narrative. Dialogue is the moment of explanation, of meaning, and to give it a place of honour would be to admit that meanings exist. M. Camus irons out the dialogue, summarizes it, renders it frequently as indirect discourse. He denies it any typographic privileges, so that a spoken phrase seems like any other happening. It flashes for an instant and then disappears, like heat lightning. Thus, when you start reading the book you feel as if you were listening to a monotonous, nasal, Arab chant rather than reading a novel. You may think that the novel is going to be like one of those tunes of which Courteline remarked that "they disappear, never to return" and stop all of a sudden. But the work gradually organizes itself before the reader's eyes and reveals its solid substructure.

There is not a single unnecessary detail, not one that is not returned to later on and used in the argument. And when we close the book, we realize that it could not have had any other ending. In this world that has been stripped of its causality and presented as absurd, the smallest incident has weight. There is no single one which does not help to lead the hero to crime and capital punishment. *The Outsider* is a classical work, an orderly work, composed about the absurd and against the absurd. Is this quite what the author was aiming at? I do not know. I am simply presenting the reader's opinion.

How are we to classify this clear, dry work, so carefully composed beneath its seeming disorder, so "human", so open, too, once you have the key? It cannot be called a story, for a story explains and co-ordinates as it narrates. It substitutes the order of causality for chronological sequence. M. Camus calls it a "novel". The novel, however, requires continuous duration, development and the manifest presence of the irreversibility of time. I would hesitate somewhat to use the term "novel" for this succession of inert present moments which allows us to see, from underneath, the mechanical economy of something deliberately staged. Or, if it is a novel, it is so in the sense that *Zadig* and *Candide* are novels. It might be regarded as a moralist's short novel, one with a discreet touch of satire and a series of ironic portraits,[1] a novel that, for all the influence of the German existentialists and the American novelists, remains, at bottom, very close to the tales of Voltaire.

(February 1943)

Those of the pimp, the judge, the prosecuting attorney, etc.

III

Jean Giraudoux

AND THE PHILOSOPHY OF ARISTOTLE

EVERYTHING we know about M. Giraudoux leads us to believe he is "normal", in the most popular as well as in the highest sense of the word. In addition, his critical studies have enabled us to appreciate the subtle delicacy of his intelligence. Nevertheless, immediately upon opening one of his novels, we feel as though we were entering the private universe of one of those waking dreamers known medically as "schizophrenics", who are characterized, as we know, by the inability to adjust to reality.

M. Giraudoux assumes and artfully elaborates all the main characteristics of these patients, their rigidity, their attempts to deny the reality of change and to refuse to recognize the present, their geometrical mentality, their fondness for symmetry, generalizations, symbols and magical communication across time and space. These qualities constitute the charm of his books. I have often been intrigued by the contrast between the man and his work. Could it be that M. Giraudoux has been amusing himself by playing the schizophrenic?

Choix des Elues, which appeared in this very review,[1] seemed to me a valuable book because it provided an answer to this question. It is certainly not M. Giraudoux's best work. But just because many of his charming devices have developed, in this book, into mechanical tricks, I found it easier to grasp the turn of this curious mind. I realized, first of all, that I had been diverted from the true interpretation of his works by a prejudice which I no doubt shared with many of his readers. Until now, I had always tried to *translate* his books. By this I mean that I proceeded on the assumption that M. Giraudoux had accumulated a great many observations, had extracted a certain wisdom from them, and then, out of a fondness for a

---

[1] *Nouvelle Revue Francaise*, March, 1940.

certain preciosity, had used a code language to express this experience and wisdom. These attempts at decoding had never been very fruitful. M. Giraudoux's depth is real, but it is valid for his world, not for ours.

And so this time I did not want to translate. I did not look for the metaphor or the symbol or the implication. I took it all at face value, with the aim of acquiring a deeper understanding, not of men, but of M. Giraudoux. In order to enter fully into the universe of *Choix des Elues*, we must first forget the world in which we live. I therefore pretended that I knew nothing at all about this soft, pasty substance traversed by waves whose cause and purpose are exterior to themselves, this world without a future, in which things are always meeting, in which the present creeps up like a thief, in which events have a natural resistance to thought and language, this world in which individuals are accidents, mere pebbles, for which the mind subsequently fabricates general categories.

I was not wrong. In the America of Edmée, Claudie and Pierre, rest and order come first. They are the goal of change and its only justification. These clear little states of rest struck me from the very beginning of the book. The book is composed of rests. A jar of pickles is not the fortuitous aspect assumed by a dance of atoms; it is a state of rest, a form closed in upon itself. A scientist's head, filled with laws and calculations, is another such rest, as is the painter's head which lies lightly on the lap of a beautiful, motionless woman, as is a landscape, a park, and even a fleeting morning light.

These ends, these limits assigned to the evolution of matter, we shall call, in medieval fashion, "substantial forms". M. Giraudoux's mind is such that the first thing he perceives is the species in the individual, and thought in matter: "A truth which was Edmée's face", he writes. That is how things are in his universe; first come truths, first come ideas and meanings that choose their own signs. "Jacques, like an *artless little boy*, with his reticence in joy and sorrow alike, had immediately turned his head aside." This little Jacques is not, to begin with, an accident, a cluster of proliferating cells; he is the embodiment of a truth. The occasion, the hour, the blue of the sky are such that a certain Jacques is meant to represent the truth common to artless little boys in a certain part of America. But this "substantial form" is independent of its embodiments, and many other little boys in many other places look away in order not to see their mothers' tears. We might say, as the schoolmen did, that in this case matter is the individualizing element. Hence this curious fondness of M. Giraudoux for universal judgments: "All the clocks in the town were ringing ten . . . All the roosters . . . All the villages in France . . ." This is not a matter of schizophrenia. These generalizations, which are tiresome in the evolving world where they would be merely an inventory of chance encounters, correspond here to those exhaustive reviews of all the children meant to embody the "artless little boy" and of all the nickel and enamel cylinders supposed to embody the "clock".

These lists generally end with the mention of an exceptional case, an oddity. "They lunched on the bank . . . feeding the birds with their crumbs, except for one bird, a suspicious fellow who had come to look at them and not to eat, and who flew away during the dessert to deliver a report somewhere." This is what we might term the playfulness of M. Giraudoux. He uses it skilfully; the general survey with the poetic or charming or comic exception is one of his most familiar devices. But this disrespect toward the established order can have significance only in relation to that order. In the work of M. Giraudoux, as in the proverb, the exception exists only in order to prove the rule.

It would be a mistake, however, to regard M. Giraudoux as a Platonist. His forms are not in the heaven of ideas, but among us, inseparable from the matter whose movements they govern. They are stamped on our skin like seals in glass. Nor are they to be confused with simple concepts. A concept contains barely more than a handful of the traits common to all the individuals of a given group. Actually, M. Giraudoux's forms contain no more, but the features that compose them are all perfect. They are norms and canons rather than general ideas. There can be no doubt but that Jacques applies spontaneously, and without even thinking about them, all the rules which enable him to make of himself the perfection of the artless little boy.

The very gesture which created Pierre has made him the most perfect realization of the scientist-husband. "Edmée's dogs, so *definitely canine*," writes M. Giraudoux. And further on: "Jacques, in order to watch over his mother, had assumed Jacques' most touching form." Or again: "The annoying thing about Pierre was that by dint of wanting to represent humanity, he had actually managed to do so. Each of his gestures, each of his words, was only the valid sample of human language and movement." So it is with all of M. Giraudoux's creatures. His books are samplings. Socrates, when questioned by Parmenides, hesitated to admit that there might be an Idea of filth, an Idea of the louse. But M. Giraudoux would not hesitate. The lice with which he is concerned are admirable in that each one represents the perfection of the louse—and each to the same degree, though in different ways.

That is why these substantial forms deserve to be called archetypes, a name which the author himself occasionally employs, rather than concepts. "Pierre looked at Edmée and drew back so as to see only her archetype." But there are also individual perfections. Edmée, who, of all mothers is the most definitely a mother—like all mothers—and of all wives the most definitely a wife—like all wives—is also the most definitely and most perfectly Edmée. And even among pickles, which, for the most part limit themselves resignedly to realizing the perfect type of the pickle, a few rare, privileged ones are, nevertheless, provided with a special archetype:

She went to get a pickle. Although one does not choose a pickle, she obeyed and took the one which, by virtue of its architecture, sculpture and relief, had the best claim to the title of pickle of the head of a household.

The world of *Choix des Elues* is a botanical atlas in which all the species are carefully classified, in which the periwinkle is blue because it is a periwinkle and the oleanders are pink because they are oleanders. Its only causality is that of the archetype. Determinism, that is, the causative action of the preceding state, is completely foreign to this world. But you will never find an *event* in it either, if by event you mean the irruption of a new phenomenon whose very novelty exceeds all expectation and upsets the conceptual order. There is almost no change, except that of matter as it is acted upon by form.

And the action of this form is of two kinds. It can act by *virtue*, like the fire of the Schoolmen which burned because of phlogiston. In this case, it takes root in matter and fashions and directs it at will. The movement is merely the temporal development of the archetype. That is why most of the gestures made in *Choix des Elues* are the gestures of madmen. The characters and objects merely realize their substantial forms in stricter fashion, the former by their acts and the latter by their changes.

No danger floated about these heads, which shone and signalled to happiness like beacons, *each with its own luminous system*. Pierre, the husband, with his two smiles, one big and one little, which followed within a second of each other every minute; Jacques, the son, with his very face, which he raised and lowered; Claudie, the daughter, a more sensitive beacon, with the fluttering of her eyelids.

Thus, the various changes in this universe, which we must reluctantly call events, are always symbols of the forms that produce them. But the form may also operate through elective affinity, whence the title: *Choix des Elues (Choice of the Elect)*.

There is not one of M. Giraudoux's creatures who is not one of the "elect". A form, lurking in the future, lies in wait for its substance; it has elected it; it draws it unto itself. And that is the second kind of change: a brief transition from one form to another, an evolution narrowly defined by its original and final terms. The bud is a state of rest; its flower is in a state of arrest; and between these two states of rest there is a directed change, the only contingency in this orderly world, a necessary and inexpressible shock. About this evolution itself there is nothing to say, and M. Giraudoux speaks of it as little as possible. Nevertheless, the subject of *Choix des Elues* is an evolution, the evolution of Edmée, the chosen one. But M. Giraudoux presents only its stages. Each of his chapters is a "stasis": Edmée at her birthday dinner, Edmée at night, a description of Claudie, Edmée at Frank's, sitting quietly with the weight of a light head on her lap; Edmée in the park, "outside time", Edmée at the Leeds', and so on.

The transitions take place behind the scenes, like the murders in Corneille. Now we understand that air of schizophrenia in M. Giraudoux's world which struck us earlier. It is a world without any present indicative. The noisy and unshapely present of surprises and catastrophes has shrunk and faded; it goes by quickly and tactfully, excusing itself as it passes. There are, to be sure, a few scenes and gestures here and there that are "performed", a few adventures that "happen". But these are all more than half generalized away, for they are primarily descriptions of the symbols of certain archetypes.

While reading, we constantly lose our footing, we glide, without realizing it, from present individuality into timeless forms. Not for a moment do we ever *feel* the weight of the head resting on Edmée's lap, nor do we see this head in its frivolous and charming individuality, bathed in the light of an American springtime. But that is unimportant, since we are concerned only with determining whether it is in the nature of a scientist's head to weigh more than the wild head of an artist. The reason is that there are two presents in M. Giraudoux's work: the ignominious present of the event, which you hide as best you can, like a family taint—and the present of the archetypes, which is eternity.

These constant limitations of the developmental process naturally accentuate the discontinuous character of time. Since change is a lesser state which exists only in order to bring about a state of rest, time is no more than a succession of little jolts, a film that has been stopped. Here is how Claudie thinks about her past:

There had been a series of a hundred, a thousand little girls, who had succeeded each other day after day in order to result in today's Claudie . . . She assembled the photographs of this multitude of Claudies, Claudettes, Claudines, Clo-Clos—there had been a Clo-Clo, the farm-girl for six months—not as photographs of herself, but as a collection of family portraits.

That is what time is really like in *Choix des Elues*; it is that of a family album. You have to turn the pages, of course, but this is only a trifling disturbance, to be forgotten, between the calm dignity of two portraits.

This explains M. Giraudoux's partiality for first beginnings. "For the first time . . .", "it was the first time . . .". Perhaps no other phrase occurs more frequently in his works, and never so frequently, perhaps, as in *Choix des Elues* (see, for example, pp. 16, 32, 58, 59, 66, 68, 69, 83, 86, etc.). The reason is that in

M. Giraudoux's world, forces do not involve progression. We, in our world, ponder the past; we vainly seek origins. "When did I begin to love her?" Actually, this love never had a beginning; it came into being gradually, and by the time I finally discovered my feeling, it had already lost its freshness. But in the work of M. Giraudoux, changes are instantaneous because they obey the famous principle of "All or Nothing". When the necessary conditions have been fulfilled, the form suddenly appears and embeds itself in matter. But should it lack one element, one only, the tiniest one—nothing happens.

Thus, as we read, we are led from one beginning to another, through an awakening world. If there is any atmosphere common to *Simon le Pathétique*, *Eglantine* and *Jerome Bardini*, it is that of morning. Throughout these books, despite ageing and the dying of the day and even massacres, the sun always rises. *Electre* ends in catastrophe and at dawn. But may I venture to say that while reading *Choix des Elues*, I no longer had the impression of those enchanted dawns that Jerome and Bella chose for their meetings? I felt as though I had been condemned to an eternal morning.

The endings, like the beginnings, are absolute. Once the balance has been destroyed, the form goes away just as it came, discreetly and entirely. "Edmée was there in the light of early morning, without a wrinkle or blur on her face, and the long night which had just passed seemed even to have been subtracted from her age." Traces, wrinkles and blemishes will do for our world, but the world of M. Giraudoux is the world of regained virginities. His people share a metaphysical chastity. They make love, of course. But neither love nor maternity leaves any mark on them. The nudity of his women is certainly a nudity that is "most definitely nudity". They are nothing *but* nude, absolutely and perfectly nude, without the desires and swellings and subsidings that are foreign to the archetype of the nude. Like the film stars that Jean Prévost called "glove-skinned women", their bodies are as thoroughly scoured as Dutch kitchens, and their gleaming flesh has the freshness of a tiled floor.

This orderly house is, however, subject to the laws of magic, or rather of alchemy, for in it we find strange transmutations— in the medieval sense of the transmutation of metals—strange, remote influences. "The first week of Claudie's life was the first week for Edmée of a world without spiders, without banana peels, without red-hot curling irons." Edmée, who is about to leave her husband, is lying beside him in "a nightgown of an off-cream colour with a yoke and trimming of Valenciennes lace". The objects in the room get angry and insult her. She rushes to the bathroom and puts on a pair of Pierre's pyjamas.

The bed grew silent . . . And thus the night passed. In these two matching garments, they were like a team. People able to see in the dark might have taken them for twins, for a tandem. Gradually, the objects, beguiled by this unexpected mimicry, calmed down . . .

The following is a description of an exorcism:

Those that wanted to give Edmée white hair, loose teeth and leathery skin, tried to enter the bed alongside the wall, disguised as Claudie. She had to accept their convention, take them by Claudie's hand, lead them back to Claudie's bed, and threaten to deprive Claudie of dessert for a week. God knows they didn't care a rap! But they were bound by their disguise and had to obey.

Thus, in order to exorcise the devils who have assumed Claudie's shape, it is enough to treat them *as if* they were Claudie. What does all this mean? M. Giraudoux himself explains it to us:

With Claudie, *everything that resembled Claudie* in this low world approved of her . . . Her peace with little Claudie meant peace with everything that was not part of the everyday world, with the mineral and vegetable, with all that was great and enduring.

This is what characterises all enchantment and spells, namely, that there is an action that makes for resemblance. We must understand that in the work of M. Giraudoux resemblance is not something perceived by the mind; it is *realized*. The "like" which he uses so frequently is never intended to clarify; it reveals a substantial analogy between acts and between things. But this need not surprise us, since his universe is a Natural History.

For him, objects somehow resemble each other when they somehow share the same form. Edmée, of course, seeks peace with Claudie alone. But Claudie is precisely that which is "not part of the everyday world". Making peace with Claudie means adapting herself more closely to the form she currently embodies, to the form of "what is great", of "what endures". Thus, by drawing closer, through love of Claudie, to the perishable embodiment of an eternal archetype, Edmée thereby finds herself mysteriously in tune with all the embodiments of that archetype, with the desert, the mountains and the virgin forest. But this is *logical*, if you consider that Edmée has come to terms, once and for all, with a universal form. Magic is merely an appearance; it arises from the fact that this form is refracted through innumerable particles of matter. Whence the profound analogies M. Giraudoux likes to reveal between the most varied kinds of objects.

The presence of forms divides the universe into an infinite number of infinite regions, and in each of these regions any object, if properly examined, will inform us about all the others. In each of these regions, loving, hating or insulting any one object means loving, hating or insulting all the others. Analogies, correspondences and symbolisms, those are what constitute the marvellous for M. Giraudoux. But as with medieval magic, all this is nothing more than a strict application of the logic of the concept.

And so we are given a ready-made world, not one which makes itself. It is the world of Linnaeus and not of Lamarck, of Cuvier and not of Geoffroy Saint-Hilaire. Let us ask ourselves what place M. Giraudoux has reserved in it for Man. We can guess that it is cut to size. If we bear in mind that its magic is only an appearance, that it is due only to hyperlogicality, we shall realize that this world is, to its very core, accessible to reason. M. Giraudoux has banished every possible element of surprise or bewilderment, including evolution, development, disorder and novelty. Man, surrounded by ready-made thoughts, the reason of trees and stones, of the moon and water, has only to enumerate and contemplate. As for M. Giraudoux himself, I quite understand his affection for members of the Registry Office.

The writer, as he sees him, is merely a real-estate clerk.

Nevertheless, a rational world might be more disturbing. Think of Pascal's infinite spaces or de Vigny's Nature. There is nothing like that here, but rather an inner conformity between Man and Nature. Look at Claudie, who is like the desert, like the virgin forest. Is it not obvious that the toughness, strength and eternity of a forest or desert are also the eternity of an instant, the tender strength and the delicate toughness of a little girl? Man discovers all of Nature's archetypes within himself and, reciprocally, himself in all Nature; he stands at the crossroads of all "regions", he is the world's centre, and its symbol, like the magician's microcosm within the great Cosmos.

Note that this man, who is so comfortably installed everywhere and equally at home in Hollywood, as is Edmée, or on a desert island, as is Suzanne, has not been subjected by M. Giraudoux to any kind of determinism. His character is not the resultant of his personal history, of his stomach trouble, of a thousand and one imponderables; his character is not the product of a gradual process. On the contrary, his personal history and even his stomach trouble result from his character. That is what you call "having a destiny". Observe, for example, the terms in which Edmée tries to warn her young son against love:

'Oh, my little Jacques, haven't you ever seen yourself? Look at yourself in a mirror. It's not that you're homely. But you'll see you're a born victim, ready made. . . . You have just the kind of face made for crying with your head in the pillow, the kind of facial planes made to press against hands trembling with despair, the tall body that waits on street corners in the rain—the breast of a person who sobs without tears . . .'

For Man's character does not really differ in any way from the "essence" of the pickle. It is an archetype realized through human life by human acts and whose perfect symbol is the human body. Thus, the most perfect union of body and spirit is achieved by means of the symbol; the way is paved for characterology and the art of physiognomy. But though we have traded the psychologist's determinism for the logical necessity of essences, we do not seem to have gained much in the exchange. Of course, we no longer have psychology, if by psychology we mean a body of empirically observed laws which govern the course of our moods. But we have not chosen to be what we are; we are "possessed" by a form and can do nothing about it. Nonetheless, this form now protects us against universal determinism. There is no danger of our being diluted in the universe.

Man, as a finite and *definite* reality, is not an effect of the world, not the by-product of any blind causal series; he is "man" or "scientist-husband" or "young boy meant to suffer in love", the way a circle is a circle, and, for this reason, he stands at the zero point of first beginnings; his acts emanate from himself only. Is this freedom? It is, at least, a *certain kind* of freedom. M. Giraudoux seems, moreover, to bestow another kind of freedom on his creatures; man realizes his essence *spontaneously*. For the mineral and the vegetable, obedience is automatic. Man conforms to his archetype of his own free will; he is constantly *choosing himself* as he *is*. This, to be sure, is a one-way freedom, for if the form is not realized *by* him, it will be realized *through* him and without his aid. In order to appreciate the thinness of the line between this freedom and absolute necessity, let us compare the following two passages. Here are freedom and inspiration:

'Where can we go, Claudie, where we've never been before?'
'To Washington Park.'
Claudie never hesitated. She had a ready answer to all questions, even the most embarrassing. . . . What a happy inspiration to have chosen to come here just at the very time when parks were of no use to people.

There has obviously been an intuition, a poetic creation of a harmony between the two women and things. But in this very intuition, Claudie has been unable to keep from realizing her essence. She is the "person who never hesitates". It was of her essence to have this intuition. And now here is a case in which the harmony between the world and our archetype manifests itself through us without consulting us:

Edmée was amazed at the words that came to her own lips, for they were surprising; but she was even more amazed at the phrase's necessity than at its monstrousness.

The difference is not very great. In one case the form is realized through our will, and in the other, it spreads, as if independently, through our body. And yet this is what distinguishes man from the pickle. This fragile and intermittent freedom, which is not an end in itself but only a means, is enough to confer a duty upon us. M. Giraudoux has an ethic. Man must freely realize his finite essence, and in so doing, freely harmonize with the rest of the world. Every man is responsible for the universal harmony and should submit of his own free will to the necessity of the archetypes. When this harmony, this balance between our deepest tendencies, between mind and nature, emerges, when man stands at the centre of an orderly world, when he is "most definitely" a man in a world "most definitely" a world, M. Giraudoux's creature then receives his reward: happiness. We now perceive the character of this author's famous humanism; it is a pagan eudaemonism.

A philosophy of the concept, scholastic problems (which is the individualizing element, matter or form?), a shame-faced evolution defined as the transition from potential to act, a white magic which is simply the superficial appearance of a rigorous logicality, an ethics of balance, happiness and the golden mean—these are the elements revealed by a candid examination of *Choix des Elues*. We are a long way from the waking dreamers. But there is an even stranger surprise in store for us. For it is impossible for the reader not to recognize, from these few characteristic traits, the philosophy of Aristotle.

Was not Aristotle primarily a logician—both a logician of the concept and a magician of logic? Is it not in Aristotle that we find this tidy, finite, classified world, a world rational to the core? Was it not he who regarded knowledge as contemplation and classification? Indeed, for him, as for M. Giraudoux, man's freedom lies less in the contingency of his evolution than in the exact realization of his essence. Both of them accept first beginnings, natural places, discontinuity and the principle of "all or nothing". M. Giraudoux has written the novel of Natural History, and Aristotle its philosophy. However, Aristotle's philosophy was the only one capable of crowning the science of his time. He wanted to systematize the accumulated treasures of observation. Now, we know that observation, by its very nature, ends in classification, and classification, likewise by its very nature, is inspired by the concept. But we are at a loss to understand M. Giraudoux.

For four hundred years philosophers and scientists have been trying to break the rigid bounds of the concept; in every field they have been trying to establish the pre-eminence of free and creative judgment and to substitute continuous evolution for the fixity of species. Today, philosophy is foundering, science is leaking at every seam, ethics is going to seed. Efforts are being made everywhere to make our methods and faculty of judging as supple as possible. No one believes any longer in a pre-established conformity between men and things; no one any longer dares hope that the heart of nature is accessible to us. But suddenly, lo and behold! a fictional world makes its appearance and wins us with its indefinable charm and air of novelty. We draw closer and discover the world of Aristotle, a world that has been buried for four hundred years.

Where does this ghost come from? How could a contemporary writer have chosen, in all simplicity, to illustrate by fictional creations the views of a Greek philosopher who died three centuries before our era? I admit I don't know. No doubt we are all Aristotelians from time to time. One evening, we stroll through the streets of Paris, and suddenly things seem to stand still. This evening of all evenings is a "Paris evening". A certain little street, one of many that lead to the Sacré-Coeur, is a "Montmartre street". Time has stopped. We experience a moment of happiness, an eternity of happiness. Which of us has not had this revelation at least once? I say "revelation", but I am wrong—or rather, it is a revelation that has nothing to teach us.

What I seize on the sidewalks, on the road, on the façades of the houses, is only the concept of street as I have long since possessed it. I have an impression of knowing without knowledge, an intuition of Necessity—without necessity. This human concept, which the street and evening reflect like mirrors, dazzles me and prevents my seeing their non-human aspect, the humble and tenacious smiles of objects. What does it matter? The street is there, it ascends, it is so purely, so magnificently, a street. . . . Whereupon we stop; there is nothing more to say. These unproductive intuitions are akin to what psychologists call the illusion of false recognition rather than to a real act of contemplation.

Is this the necessary explanation of M. Giraudoux's sensibility? It would be quite a presumptuous one, and besides, I do not really know. I suppose, too, that a Marxist would term M. Giraudoux's views an urbane rationalism and that he would explain the rationalism in terms of the triumphant rise of capitalism at the beginning of this century—and the urbanity by M. Giraudoux's very special position within the French bourgeoisie—with his peasant origins, his Hellenic culture and his diplomatic career. I do not know. This discreet and self-effacing writer remains a mystery.

(March 1940.)

IV

"Aminadab"

or The Fantastic Considered as a Language

> "Thought taken ironically for an object by something
> other than thought."
> —Maurice Blanchot: *Thomas l'Obscur*

THOMAS is walking through a village. Who is Thomas? Where does he come from? Where is he going? We know nothing about him. A woman signals to him from a house. He enters and finds himself suddenly in a strange republic of tenants in which everyone seems both to rule and to be ruled. He is made to undergo incoherent initiation rites; he is chained to an almost mute companion with whom he wanders from room to room and floor to floor, frequently forgetting what he is after but always remembering just in time when someone tries to detain him.

After many adventures, he changes, loses his companion and falls ill. It is then that he receives the final warning. "It's yourself you ought to be questioning," an old clerk tells him. A nurse adds, "You've been the victim of an illusion: You thought you were being called, but there was no one. The call came from yourself." Nevertheless, he perseveres, gets to the upper storeys and finds the woman who had signalled to him, but only to be told, "There was no order summoning you: It was someone else who was expected." Thomas has been growing weaker and weaker.

At nightfall, his former companion-in-chains comes to see him and explains that he had taken the wrong direction. "You failed to recognize your path . . . I was like another self to you. I knew all the ways through the house, and I knew the one you should have followed. You had only to ask me. . . ." Thomas asks one last question, but it is never answered, and the room is invaded by the darkness from outside, "beautiful and soothing . . . an immense dream beyond the reach of the person it envelops."

When summed up in this way, M. Blanchot's intentions seem very clear. Even clearer still is the extraordinary resemblance between his book and the novels of Kafka. There is the same minute and courtly style, the same nightmare politeness, the same preposterous and studied ceremoniousness, the same vain quests that lead nowhere, the same exhaustive and useless discussions, the same sterile initiations that initiate into nothing. M. Blanchot says that at the time he wrote *Aminadab* he had not read anything of Kafka's. This leads us to wonder all the more what strange turn led this young writer, still uncertain of his style, to rediscover, in an effort to express a few banal ideas about human life, the same instrument that once gave forth such extraordinary sounds when played by other hands.

I do not know how this conjunction came about. It interests me only because it allows us to draw up the "present balance sheet" of the literature of the fantastic. For fantasy, like other literary genres, has an essence and history of its own, the latter being only the development of the former. What must the nature of the fantastic be in our time if it leads a French writer, convinced of the necessity of "thinking French",[1] to find himself, upon adopting fantasy as his mode of expression, on the same terrain as a writer of Central Europe?

In order to achieve the fantastic, it is neither necessary nor sufficient to portray extraordinary things. The strangest event will enter into the order of the universe if it is alone in a world governed by laws. If you make a horse talk, I will believe, for a moment, that he is under a spell. But if he goes on talking amidst motionless trees, on solid ground, I will take his talking for granted. I shall cease to see the horse and shall see, in its place, a man disguised as a horse. If, on the other hand, you succeed in convincing me that the horse is a creature of fantasy, then the trees, earth and river are also objects of fantasy, even if you have not said so. You cannot impose limits on the fantastic; either it does not exist at all, or else it extends throughout the universe. It is an entire world in which things manifest a captive, tormented thought, a thought both

[1] M. Blanchot was, I believe, a disciple of Charles Maurras.

whimsical and enchained, that gnaws away from below at the mechanism's links without ever managing to express itself. In this world, matter is never entirely matter, since it offers only a constantly frustrated attempt at determinism, and mind is never completely mind, because it has fallen into slavery and has been impregnated and dulled by matter. All is woe. Things suffer and tend towards inertia, without ever attaining it; the debased, enslaved mind unsuccessfully strives towards consciousness and freedom.

The fantastic presents a reverse image of the union of body and soul. In it, the soul takes the place of the body, and the body that of the soul, and we cannot use clear, distinct ideas in pondering this image. We are forced to resort to blurred thoughts which are in themselves fantastic. In short, we have to indulge, though wide awake and fully mature and in the midst of civilization, in the magical "mentality" of the dreamer, the primitive and the child. Thus, there is no need to resort to fairies. Fairies in themselves are simply pretty girls. The fantastic thing is nature when she obeys the fairies; it is nature within and outside of man, perceived like a man turned inside out.

So long as it was thought possible to escape the conditions of human existence through asceticism, mysticism, metaphysical disciplines or the practice of poetry, fantasy was called upon to fulfil a very definite function. It manifested our human power to transcend the human. Men strove to create a world that was not of this world, whether because, like Poe, one preferred the artificial on principle, or because, like Gazotte or Rimbaud and others who practised "seeing a salon at the bottom of a lake", one believed in the writer's magical mission or because, like Lewis Carroll, one was interested in a systematic application to literature of the mathematician's absolute power to beget a universe on the basis of a few conventions, or whether because, like Nodier, one had recognized that the writer was primarily a liar and so tried to attain the absolute lie.

The object thus created referred only to itself. It did not aim at portraying anything, but only at existing. It compelled recognition only through its own density. Though certain writers did borrow the language of fantasy for the expression of certain philosophical and moral ideas in the guise of entertaining stories, they readily admitted that they had diverted this mode of expression from its usual purposes and that they had only created, so to speak, an illusionist fantasy.

M. Blanchot began to write in an age of disillusion. After the long metaphysical holiday of the post-war period, which ended in disaster, the new generation of artists and writers, out of pride and humility and earnestness, had returned, with much ado, to the human. This tendency had an effect on fantasy itself. For Kafka, who figures in this context as a forerunner, a transcendental reality certainly existed, but it was beyond our reach and served only to give us a sharper feeling of man's abandonment in the realm of the human. M. Blanchot, who does not believe in transcendence, would probably agree with Eddington when he says that we have discovered a strange footprint on the shore of the Unknown and that after having constructed one theory after another to explain its origin we have finally managed to reconstruct the creature who left the footprint, and that this creature happens to be ourselves.

This accounts for the attempt at "a return to the human" in the literature of fantasy. It is certainly not going to be used to prove anything or to instruct. M. Blanchot, in particular, denies that he has written the kind of allegory in which, as he puts it, "the meaning corresponds unequivocally to the story but can also be explained apart from it". However, in order to find a place within the humanism of our time, fantasy, like other things, is going to become domesticated will give up the exploration of transcendental reality and resign itself to transcribing the human condition. Now, at about the same time and as a result of internal factors, this literary genre was pursuing its own evolution and getting rid of fairies, genii and goblins as useless and outworn conventions.

Dali and de Chirico revealed to us a nature that was haunted and yet had nothing of the supernatural about it. The former depicted a biology of horror, showing us the horrible sprouting of human bodies and of life-contaminated metals; the latter painted the life and sufferings of stones. Through a curious twist, the new humanism gave rise to a new development. After Kafka, M. Blanchot is no longer concerned with spells that have been cast on matter. He probably regards Dali's monstrosities as conventional props, just as Dali regarded haunted castles. For him there is only one fantastic object, man. Not the man of religion and of spiritualism, waist-high only in the things of this world, but man-as-he-is-given, natural man, social man, the man who removes his hat when a hearse goes by, who shaves near a window, who kneels in church, who marches in step behind a flag.

This being is a microcosm; he is the world, he is all of nature. Only in him can the totality of spellbound nature be revealed. In him, not in his body. M. Blanchot is not interested in physiological fantasies; his characters are physically *ordinary*. He characterizes them briefly, in passing, but in their total reality of *homo faber* or *homo sapiens*. Thus, the fantastic, in becoming humanized, approaches the ideal purity of its essence, becomes what it had been. It seems to be stripped of all its artifices; there is nothing in its hands or pockets. We recognize the footprint on the shore as our own. There are no phantoms, no succubi, no weeping fountains. There are only men, and the creator of the fantastic announces that he identifies himself with the fantastic object. For contemporary man, the fantastic is only one of a hundred ways of mirroring his own image.

It is on the basis of these observations that we can try for a better understanding of the extraordinary resemblance between *Aminadab* and *The Castle*. We have seen that it is of the essence of the fantastic to offer the reverse image of the union of body and soul. Now, in Kafka, as in M. Blanchot, the fantastic is limited to expressing the human world. Is it not going to be bound, in both authors, by new conditions? And what will be the significance of the inversion of human relationships?

When I enter a café, the first thing I perceive are implements. Not things, not raw matter, but utensils: tables, seats, mirrors, glasses and saucers. Each of these represents a piece of domesticated matter. Taken as a whole, they belong to an obvious order. The meaning of this ordering is an *end*—an end that is myself, or rather, the man in me, the consumer that I am. Such is the surface appearance of the human world. It would be useless for us to look for "raw material" in this world. Here the means functions as matter, and form—mental order—is represented by the end. Now let us describe the café topsy-turvy.

We will have to show ends crushed by their own means and trying vainly to pierce the enormous layers of matter or, if you prefer, objects that reveal their own instrumentality, but with an indiscipline and disorderly power, a kind of coarse independence that suddenly snatches their end from us just when we think we have it fast. Here, for example, is a door. It is there before us, with its hinges, latch and lock. It is carefully bolted, as if protecting some treasure. I manage, after several attempts, to procure a key; I open it, only to find that behind it is a wall. I sit down and order a cup of coffee. The waiter makes me repeat the order three times and repeats it himself to avoid any possibility of error. He dashes off and repeats my order to a second waiter, who notes it down in a little book and transmits it to a third waiter. Finally, a fourth waiter comes back and, putting an inkwell on my table, says, "There you are." "But," I say, "I ordered a cup of coffee." "That's right," he says, as he walks off.

If the reader, while reading a story of this kind, thinks that the waiters are playing a joke or that they are involved in some collective psychosis, then we have lost the game. But if we have been able to give him the impression that we are talking about a world in which these absurd manifestations appear as normal behaviour, then he will find himself plunged all at once into the heart of the fantastic. The fantastic is the revolt of means against ends; either the object in question noisily asserts itself as a means, concealing its end through the very violence of its assertion, or it refers back to another means, and this one to still another, and so on *ad infinitum*, without our ever being able to discover the ultimate end, or else some interference in means belonging to independent series gives us a glimpse of a composite and blurred image of contradictory ends.

Suppose, on the other hand, I finally manage to perceive an end? All the bridges have been burned; I am unable to discover or invent any method of realizing it. Someone has made an appointment to meet me on the first floor of this café; I absolutely must go upstairs. I see the first floor from below, I see its balcony through a big circular opening, I can even see tables and customers seated at these tables. But though I walk all round the room any number of times, I cannot find the stairs. The means in this case is precise; everything in the situation indicates and requires it; it is latent in the manifest presence of the end.

But it has carried the prank to the point of self-annihilation. Am I to call this world "absurd", as M. Camus does in *The Outsider*? But absurdity means the complete absence of ends. The absurd is the object of clear and distinct thought. It belongs to the right-side-up world, as the actual limit of human powers. In the eccentric and hallucinating world we are trying to describe, the absurd would be an oasis, a respite, and thus there is no place for it. I cannot stop there for an instant; each means refers me constantly to the phantom end by which it is haunted, and each end sends me back to the phantom means through which I might bring about its realization. I am unable to think at all, except in terms of slippery and iridescent notions that disintegrate as I behold them.

It is therefore not surprising to find rigorously identical themes in writers so different from each other as Kafka and Blanchot. They are both trying to depict the same preposterous world. They are primarily concerned with excluding "impassive Nature", and that is why we find the same stifling atmosphere in the novels of both men. The hero of *The Trial* struggles in a great city; he walks through streets and enters houses. Thomas, in *Aminadab*, wanders through the endless corridors of an apartment building. Neither of them ever gets a glimpse of forests, plains and hills. How restful it would be if they could come within sight of a mound of earth or a useless piece of matter! But if they did, the fantastic would immediately vanish; the law of this genre condemns it to encounter instruments only. These instruments are not, as we have seen, meant to serve them, but rather to manifest unremittingly an evasive, preposterous finality. This accounts for the labyrinth of corridors, doors and staircases that lead to nothing, the signposts that point to nothing, the innumerable signs that line the roads and that mean nothing. As a particular instance of the theme of the sign, let us take the motif of the message, which is so important in the work of both M. Blanchot and Kafka. In the "right-side-up" world, a message presupposes a sender, a messenger and a recipient. It has only the value of a means; its end is its contents. In the "topsy-turvy" world, the means is isolated and is posed for its own sake. We are plagued by messages without content, without messenger and without sender. Or the end may even exist, but the means will gradually eat it away.

In one of Kafka's stories, the emperor sends a message to someone who lives in the city, but the messenger has such a long way to go that the message never reaches its destination. M. Blanchot tells us of a message whose contents are progressively changed in the course of the journey. "All these hypotheses," he writes, "make probable the following conclusion: that when the messenger finally gets there, he will, for all his good intentions, have forgotten his message and will be unable to transmit it. Or, granting that he has scrupulously retained the terms of the message, it will be impossible for him to know what it means, for what had meaning here must necessarily have a completely different one or none at all there. . . . I refuse to imagine what will have become of the messenger himself, for I presume that he would seem as different from what I am as the message to be transmitted must be from the one received." It is also possible for a message to reach us and be partly decipherable. But we learn later that it was not meant for us.

In *Aminadab*, M. Blanchot discovers another possibility: a message comes to me which is, of course, incomprehensible; I undertake an investigation and learn, finally, that the sender was myself. Needless to say, these possibilities do not represent a few strokes of bad luck amidst many others. They are part of the *nature* of the message. The sender knows this, the recipient is not unaware of it, and still they continue untiringly, the former to send letters and the latter to receive them, as if the important thing were the message itself and not its content. The means has absorbed the end as the blotter absorbs ink.

The same reasoning which leads our two authors to exclude nature from their stories also leads them to exclude natural man, that is, the isolated person, the individual, the man Celine calls "a fellow", of no collective importance who can be only an absolute end. The fantastic imperative inverts the Kantian imperative. "Always act in such a way", it tells us, "that you treat the human in yourself and in others as a means and never as an end." In order to plunge their heroes into a feverish, harassing, unintelligible activity, M. Blanchot and Kafka have to surround them with men who are instruments. The reader, referred from the implement to the man, as from means to end, discovers that man is, in turn, only a means. This accounts for the civil servants and soldiers and judges who throng Kafka's books, and for the servants, who are also called "employees", who fill *Aminadab*.

As a result, the universe of the fantastic seems like a bureaucracy. Actually, it is the civil service that most resembles a "topsy-turvy" society. Thomas, in *Aminadab*, goes from office to office, from employee to employee, without ever finding either the employer or the director, like the visitors who have requests to make at a government office and who are sent endlessly from one department to another. Besides, the actions of these civil servants remain utterly unintelligible. In the right-side-up world I can distinguish fairly well between the magistrate's sneezing, which is an accident, or his whistling, which is an idiosyncrasy, and his juridical activity, which is the application of the law.

Let us reverse things: the fantastic employees, who are careful and even finical, will seem to me, at first, to be carrying out their functions diligently. But I shall soon learn that this zeal is utterly meaningless, or that it is even wrong; it is a mere caprice. The hasty gesture, on the other hand, which shocks me by its incongruity, proves, upon further examination, to be in perfect conformity with the social dignity of the character; it was performed according to law. Thus, law disintegrates into whim, and whim gives us a sudden insight into law. In vain would I demand codes, rules or decrees; old orders lie about on the desks and the employees conform to them without anyone's being able to know whether these orders have been issued by someone in authority or whether they are the product of an anonymous and time-honoured routine or whether they are not the inventions of the civil servants.

Their very scope is ambiguous, and I shall never be able to decide whether they apply to all members of the community or whether they concern only myself. Nevertheless, this ambiguous law that wavers between rule and caprice, between the universal and the particular, is omnipresent. It hems you in, it overwhelms you. You are violating it when you think you are following it, and when you rebel against it, you find yourself obeying it unknowingly. No one is supposed to be ignorant of it, and yet no one knows what it is. Its aim is not to keep order nor regulate human relationships. It is the Law, purposeless, meaningless and without content, and none can escape it.

But now we must tie things together. No one can penetrate the universe of dreams except in sleep. In like manner, no one can enter the world of the fantastic except by becoming fantastic. We know that the reader begins his reading by identifying himself with the hero of the novel. Thus, the hero, by lending us his point of view, constitutes the sole way of access to the fantastic. The old technique presented him as a man right-side up, transported miraculously into an upside-down world.

Kafka used this method at least once. Joseph K., in *The Trial*, is a normal man. The advantage of this technique is apparent. It sets off, by contrast, the strange character of the new world; the fantastic novel becomes an "Erziehungsroman". The reader shares the hero's astonishment and follows him from discovery to discovery. However, he thereby sees the fantastic *from the outside*, as a spectacle, as if waking reason were peacefully contemplating the images of our dreams. In *The Castle* Kafka perfected his technique; the hero himself is fantastic. We know nothing about this surveyor whose adventures and views we share. We know nothing except his incomprehensible obstinacy in remaining in a forbidden village. To attain this end, he sacrifices everything; he treats himself as a means. But we never know the value this end had for him and whether it was worth so much effort.

M. Blanchot has adopted the same method; his Thomas is no less mysterious than the servants in the building. We do not know where he comes from, nor why he persists in reaching the woman who has signalled to him. Like Kafka, like Samsa, like the Surveyor, Thomas is *never surprised*; he becomes outraged, as though the succession of events he witnesses seem to him perfectly natural, but blameworthy, as though he possessed within himself a strange standard of Good and Evil of which M. Blanchot has carefully omitted to inform us.

We are thus forced, by the very laws of the novel, to assume a point of view which is not our own, to condemn without understanding and to contemplate without surprise that which amazes us. In addition, M. Blanchot opens and closes his hero's mind as though it were a box. Sometimes we enter it, and at other times we are left outside at the door. And when we are inside, it is only to find lines of reasoning already begun, that link up like mechanisms and presuppose principles and ends unknown to us. We fall into step; since we *are* the hero, we keep step with his reasoning. But these speeches never lead to anything, as if the important thing were merely to reason. Once again the means has devoured the end. And our reason, which should have set the world to rights, is pulled into this nightmare and itself becomes fantastic. M. Blanchot has gone even further. In an excellent passage in *Aminadab*, his hero suddenly discovers that he is unknowingly employed in the house and that he is fulfilling the functions of executioner.

Thus, we have been patiently questioning the officials, for they seemed to us to know the law and the secrets of the universe. And now we suddenly learn that we ourselves were civil servants without being aware of it. And now the others look at us imploringly and question us in turn. Perhaps we do know the law, after all. "Knowing," said Alain, "consists in knowing that one knows." But that is a maxim that belongs to the right-side-up world. In the topsy-turvy world, one is unaware of knowing what one knows; and when one knows that one knows, then one does not know. Thus, our last resource, that self-awareness in which stoicism sought refuge, escapes us and disintegrates. Its transparence is that of the void, and our being is outside, in the hands of others.

Such, in their main features, are the principal themes of *The Castle* and *Aminadab*. I hope I have demonstrated that they were imperative from the moment one chose to paint the world upside-down. But the question may arise as to why it was necessary to paint it upside-down. What a silly thing to do —to describe man by standing him on his head! In actual fact, it is quite true that this world is not fantastic, for the simple reason that everything in it is right-side up. A horror novel can be regarded as a simple transposition of reality because in the course of our lives we do meet with terrible situations. But, as we have seen, there would be no fantastic incidents in it, since the fantastic can exist only as a universe. Let us look into the matter a little more closely. If I am upside-down in a world that is upside-down, then everything seems right-side up to me. If, then, I were fantastic myself and inhabited a fantastic world, I should be unable to regard it as fantastic. This will help us to understand our author's intentions.

Thus, I cannot judge this world, since my judgments are part of it. If I conceive of it as a work of art or as a piece of complicated clockwork, I do so by means of human notions; if, on the other hand, I declare it to be absurd, I do so likewise by means of human concepts. As to the ends pursued by our species, how are they to be described unless in relation to other ends? I can, if need be, hope to know eventually the details of the mechanism that surrounds me, but how is man to judge the entire world, that is, the world with man inside it? Yet I would like to know the underside of the cards, I want to contemplate mankind as it is. The artist persists where the philosopher has given up. He invents convenient fictions to satisfy us: Micromegas, the noble savage, Riquet the dog, or that "Outsider" of whom M. Camus has recently been speaking. These are pure beholders who escape the human condition and can thereby inspect it. In the eyes of these angels, the human world is a *given* reality. They can say that it is this or that and that it could be otherwise. Human ends are contingent; they are simple facts which the angels regard as we regard the ends of bees and ants.

Man's progress is simply a matter of marking time, since he can no more get out of this finite and limitless world than the ant can escape from its ant's universe. However, by forcing the reader to identify himself with an inhuman hero, we make him soar like a bird above the human condition. He escapes, he loses sight of that prime necessity of the universe he is contemplating, that is the fact that man is inside it. How is one to make him see *from the outside* this obligation to be inside? Such is, fundamentally, the problem posed for Blanchot and Kafka. It is an exclusively literary and technical problem and would retain no meaning on the philosophical level.

Here is the solution they have found: they have eliminated the angels' gaze and have plunged the reader into the world with K. and Thomas; but they have left, as it were, a ghost of transcendence, floating about within this immanence. The implements, acts and ends are all familiar to us, and we are on such intimate terms with them that we hardly notice them. But just when we feel shut up with them in a warm atmosphere of organic sympathy, they are presented to us in a cold, strange light. This brush is here in my hand. I have only to take it in order to brush my clothes. But just as I touch it, I stop. It is a brush seen from the outside; it is there, in all its contingency; it refers back to contingent ends, just as the white pebble which the ant stupidly drags towards its hole appears to human eyes. "They brush their clothes every morning," the Angel would say. It would require little more to make this activity seem eccentric and unintelligible.

There is no angel in M. Blanchot's book, but, on the other hand, he tries to make us see *our* ends—those ends which are born of us and which give meaning to our lives—as *ends for other people.* We are shown only the external side of those alienated, petrified ends, the side facing outwards, the side which makes *facts* of them. They are petrified ends, underhand ends, invaded by materiality, ends that are observed before they are wanted. As a result, the means takes on an independent existence. If it is no longer taken for granted that one must brush oneself every morning, the brush seems an undecipherable implement, the wreckage of a civilization that has disappeared. It still has a certain meaning, like the pipe-shaped tools that were found at Pompeii. But we no longer know what they mean. What are those immobilized ends, these monstrous and powerless means, if they are not the universe of the fantastic?

The method is clear: since human activity seems reversed when seen from the outside, Kafka and M. Blanchot, in order to make us see our condition from the outside without resorting to angels, have painted a world that is topsy-turvy. It is a contradictory world in which mind becomes matter, since values look like facts, a world in which matter is eaten away by mind, since everything is both ends and means, a world in which, without ceasing to be within, I see myself from without. Better still, we cannot ponder it at all.

That is the reason why M. Blanchot writes: "The meaning can be grasped only through a fiction and melts away as soon as we try to understand it for itself. . . . The story . . . seems mysterious because it tells everything about something that will not bear telling." There is a sort of marginal existence of the fantastic. Look at it squarely. Try to express its meaning with words. It immediately disappears, for, after all, one must be either inside or out. But if you read the story without trying to translate it, it attacks you by the flank.

The few truths that you will extract from *Aminadab* will lose their colour and their life once they are out of the water. Yes, of course, man is alone in the world, he alone decides his destiny, he himself invents the law to which he is subject; each of us is a stranger to himself and a victim and executioner for everyone else; we do seek in vain to transcend man's estate, we would do better to acquire a Nietzschean sense of the earth. Yes, to be sure, M. Blanchot's wisdom seems to belong to those "transcendances" of which Jean Wahl has spoken in connection with Heidegger. But after all, none of this sounds very new. Yet, when these truths wove in and out of the narrative, they shone with a strange brilliance. And they did so because we were seeing them wrong-side out; they were fantastic truths.

Our authors, who have gone such a long way together, part company here. About Kafka I have nothing more to say, except that he is one of the greatest and most unique writers of our time. And besides, he was the first on the scene; the technique he chose corresponded in him to a need. If he shows us human life everlastingly troubled by an impossible transcendence, it is because he believes in the existence of this transcendence. Only, it is beyond our reach. His universe is both fantastic and rigorously true. M. Blanchot has certainly a considerable talent. But he came afterwards, and the artifices he employs are already too familiar.

In commenting on Jean Paulhan's *Les Fleurs de Tarbes* he wrote, "Those writers who had, through prodigies of asceticism the illusion of standing apart from all literature, because they wanted to rid themselves of conventions and forms in order to make direct contact with the secret world and the deeper metaphysics that they wished to reveal . . . finally contented themselves with using this world, this secret and this metaphysics as conventions and forms which they revealed with a certain casualness and which constituted both the visible structure and the content of their works. . . . For this sort of writer, metaphysics, religion and feelings take the place of language and technique. They are a system of expression, a literary form, in a word, literature."[1]

I am really afraid that this reproach, if it is a reproach, can be turned against M. Blanchot himself. The system of signs which he has chosen does not quite correspond to the thought he is expressing. There was no need to resort to artifices which introduce an external view into consciousness in order to depict "the nature of spirit, its deep split, this struggle of the Same with the Same, which is the means of its power, its torment and its apotheosis."[2] I am inclined to say of M. Blanchot what Lagneau said of Barrès, that he has misused the tool. And this slight discrepancy between the sign and the thing signified turns the deeply experienced themes of Kafka into literary conventions. Thanks to M. Blanchot there is now a "Kafkaesque" stereotype of the fantastic, just as there is a stereotype of haunted castles and stuffed monsters. I am aware that art thrives on conventions, but one must at least know how to choose them. Seen against a transcendence tinged with Maurrassianism, the fantastic gives an effect of having been laid on.

This uneasy feeling on the part of the reader is heightened by the fact that M. Blanchot does not remain faithful to his purpose. He had told us that he hopes that the meaning of *Aminadab* "vanishes as soon as one tries to understand it for itself". Very well, but in that case, why offer us a continual translation, a full commentary on its symbols? In many passages the explanations become so insistent that the story very clearly takes on the aspect of an allegory. Let us choose at random a page from the long account which develops the myth of the servants, for example the following: "I warned you that the staff was invisible most of the time. Such a remark was stupid, a proud temptation to which I yielded and for which I blush. Is the staff invisible? Is it invisible most of the time? But we never see the staff, we never get a glimpse of it, even from afar; we do not even know what the word *see* can mean as regards the staff, nor whether there is a word to express its absence, nor whether the thought of this absence is not an

[1] *Comment la littérature est elle possible?* (José Corti), p. 23.
[2] *Ibid.*

ultimate and disheartening means of making us imagine its arrival.

"The state of negligence in which it keeps us is, in certain ways, unimaginable. Since many people have had their health ruined or have paid with their lives for its inadequate service, we might, then, complain about its apparent indifference to our interests. Still, we should be ready to forgive everything if it gave us some satisfaction now and then. . . ."[1] Replace the word "staff" in the passage by "God" and the word "service" by "Providence", and you will have a perfectly comprehensible statement of a certain aspect of religious feeling. Often, too, the objects in this falsely fantastic world yield their meaning to us "right-side up", without needing any commentary, like the companion-in-chains who is so obviously the body, the humiliated body, mistreated in a society which has declared a divorce between the physical and the spiritual. We then feel as if we were translating a translation, as if we were rendering a text into our native language.

Moreover, I do not pretend to have grasped all the author's intentions and perhaps I have misunderstood a number of them. The fact that these intentions, even when obscure, were obvious, was enough to trouble me. I still think that with more effort or more intelligence I could have cleared them all up. In Kafka, the accidents link up in accordance with the necessities of the plot. In *The Trial*, for example, never for a moment do we lose sight of the fact that K. is struggling to defend his honourable character, his life. But why is Thomas struggling? He has no definite character, he has no purpose, he hardly interests us. And the events accumulate haphazardly. "As they do in life," someone may object. But life is not a novel, and the series of happenings without rhyme or reason that can be drawn from the novel turn our attention, in spite of ourselves, to the secret intentions of the author.

Why does Thomas lose his companion-in-chains and fall ill? Nothing in this upside-down world either prepares for or explains his illness. This means, then, that the reason for it lies outside this world, in the providential intentions of the author. Thus most of the time M. Blanchot is wasting his effort. He does not succeed in ensnaring the reader in the nightmarish world he is

[1] *Aminadab*, p. 95.

portraying. The reader escapes; he is outside—outside with the author himself. He contemplates these dreams as he would a well-assembled machine.

He loses his footing only at rare moments. These moments are, moreover, enough to reveal in M. Blanchot a writer of quality. He is subtle and ingenious, at times profound. He has a love of words; he needs only to find his style. His venture into the fantastic is not without consequence, for it helps us to determine our bearings. Kafka could not be imitated; he remained on the horizon like a perpetual temptation. By having unwittingly imitated him, M. Blanchot delivers us from him. He brings his methods into the open. They are now catalogued, classified, fixed and useless, and no longer frightening or dizzying. Kafka was only a stage on the way. Through him, as through Hoffmann, Poe, Lewis Carroll and the surrealists, the fantastic pursues the continuous progress which should ultimately reunite it with what it has always been.

V

William Faulkner's "Sartoris"

WITH a little perspective, good novels come almost to resemble natural phenomena. We forget that they have authors; we accept them as we do stones or trees, because they are there, because they exist. *Light in August* was just such an hermetic thing, a mineral. We do not accept *Sartoris*, and that is what makes the book so precious. Faulkner betrays himself in it; we catch him red-handed all the way through. This book led me to an understanding of the mainspring of Faulkner's art. This mainspring is illusion. It is true that all art is false. Paintings lie about perspective. There are, however, two kinds of pictures: real pictures and the illusionist kind.

I had accepted the "Man" of *Light in August*. (I thought of him as "Faulknerian Man", the way one thinks of Dostoievskian or Meredithian Man.) I had accepted this big, Godless, divine animal, lost from birth and bent on self-destruction, moral even in murder and redeemed—not by or in death, but in his last moments before death. I had accepted this animal, who is great even in torture and in the most abject humiliation of the flesh. I had accepted him uncritically. I had not forgotten his haughty, threatening, tyrant's visage, nor his sightless eyes. I found him again in *Sartoris*. I recognized Bayard's "gloomy arrogance".

And yet I can no longer accept Faulkner's Man; he is an illusionist creation. It is all done with lighting. There is a trick, and the trick lies in not telling, in keeping secrets—surreptitiously; in telling *just a little*. We are told that old Bayard is upset over the unexpected return of his grandson. We are told surreptitiously, however, in a half-phrase that might almost pass unnoticed, and which Faulkner hopes will pass *almost* unnoticed. Then, when we are expecting stormy outbreaks, we are given a minute and lengthy description of his gestures.

Faulkner is not unaware of our impatience; he counts on it and stops there, to chat innocently of gestures. There have been other chatterers, the realists, for example, Dreiser. But Dreiser's descriptions are informative; they are documentary. Here, the gestures (drawing on boots, climbing a staircase, mounting a horse) have no descriptive purpose, but are intended to conceal things. We watch for something to betray Bayard's agitation, but the Sartorises never get drunk, never betray themselves through gestures. Nevertheless, these idols, whose gestures have something of a ritual-like threat about them, also possess consciousnesses.

They talk, they think to themselves, they become aroused. Faulkner knows this. Now and then he casually reveals a consciousness to us. But it is like a conjurer holding up the box when it is empty. What do we see? Only gestures, no more than we could see from the outside. Or else, we take a relaxed consciousness by surprise as it is falling asleep, and once again we find gestures, tennis, piano, whisky or conversation. And that is what I cannot accept. Everything is aimed at making us believe that these minds are always empty and evasive. Why? Because a consciousness is too human a thing. Aztec Gods do not engage in pleasant little conversations with themselves. But Faulkner knows perfectly well that minds are not and *cannot* be empty. He knows this well enough to write:

. . . she again held her consciousness submerged deliberately deliberately, as you hold a puppy under water until its struggles cease.

But he does not tell us what is *inside* the consciousness he wants to drown. Not exactly that he wants to conceal it. He hopes we will guess it, because whatever is touched by divination becomes magical. And the gestures begin all over again. We feel like complaining of "too many gestures", just as someone told Mozart that his score had "too many notes". There are, also, too many words. Faulkner's volubility, his lofty, abstract, anthropomorphic, preacher's style are still other illusionist devices. The style clogs the everyday gestures, weighs them down, encumbers them with an epic magnificence and makes them sink, like clay pigeons. This is done intentionally. Faulkner is actually aiming at just this pompous, sickening monotony, this ritual of everyday life.

The gestures imply a world of boredom. These rich people, decent and uncultivated, who have neither work nor leisure, prisoners on their own land, masters enslaved to their own negroes, try to fill in the time with gestures. But this boredom (has Faulkner always managed to distinguish between his heroes' boredom and that of his readers?) is only an appearance; it is Faulkner's defence against us, and the Sartorises' defence against themselves. The boredom is in the social order, the monotonous languor of everything they can see, hear or touch. Faulkner's landscapes are as bored as his characters.

The real drama is *behind*, behind the boredom, behind the gestures, behind the characters' consciousness. Suddenly, from the depths of this drama, like a bolt from the blue, appears the Act. At last, an act! something *happening*, a message! But Faulkner disappoints us again; he rarely describes acts, because he encounters and by-passes an old problem of fictional technique. Acts are of the essence of the novel. They are carefully prepared, and then, by the time they happen, they are utterly simple, as smooth and polished as bronze. They slip between our fingers. There is nothing more to say about them; the mere mention of them suffices. Faulkner does not speak of acts, never mentions them, and thus suggests that there is no naming them, that they are beyond language. He shows only their results: an old man, dead in his seat, a car turned over in the river and two feet sticking out of the water. These brutal and static consequences, as solid and compact as the Act is fleeting, appear amidst the fine, close rain of everyday gestures to flaunt themselves in their inexplicable finality.

These undecipherable acts of violence will later change into "stories"; they will be given names, will be analysed and re-counted. All these men, all these families, have their stories. The Sartoris family carries the heavy burden of two wars and of two series of stories, the Civil War, in which Bayard, the ancestor, died, and the World War, in which John Sartoris died. The stories appear and disappear, passing from mouth to mouth, dragging on along with the gestures of everyday life. They do not belong completely to the past; they are, rather, a super-present.

As usual, old man Falls had brought John Sartoris into the room with him . . . Freed as he was of time and flesh, he was a far more palpable presence than either of the other two old men who sat shouting periodically into one another's deafness . . .

They constitute the poetry and fatality of the present: "fatal immortality and immortal fatality". It is with these stories that Faulkner's heroes forge their destinies. A nameless act, buried for years, beckons, through tales that have been embellished by generations, to other Acts, charming and attracting them, as a rod attracts lightning. Such is the subtle power of stories and words. Yet, Faulkner does not believe in these incantations:

What had been a hare-brained prank of two heedless and reckless boys wild with their own youth had become a gallant and finely tragical focal point to which the history of the race had been raised . . . by two angels valiantly fallen and strayed, altering the course of human events . . .

He never allows himself to be entirely taken in. He knows these tales for what they are worth, since it is he who is telling them, since he, like Sherwood Anderson, is "a story-teller, an inventor". But he dreams of a world in which the stories would be believed, in which they would really affect men, and his novels depict the world of his dreams. We are familiar with the "technique of disorder" of *The Sound and the Fury* and of *Light in August*, those inextricable mixtures of past and present. I thought I had found their twofold origin in *Sartoris*. On the one hand, there is the irresistible need to interrupt the action in order to relate a story. This seems to me characteristic of many lyrical novelists. And, on the other hand, there is that half-sincere, half-imaginary faith in the magical power of stories. But when Faulkner wrote *Sartoris*, he had not yet perfected his technique; the transitions from present to past and from gesture to story are very clumsily managed.

This, then, is man as Faulkner asks us to accept him. Faulkner's man is *undiscoverable*. He is to be understood neither in terms of his gestures, which are a façade, nor through his tales, which are imaginary, nor yet by his acts, for they are lightning flashes that defy description. And yet, beyond behaviour and beyond words, beyond empty consciousness, Man exists. We have an inkling of a genuine drama, a kind of intelligible nature that might explain everything. But just what is this nature? Is it a racial or family taint, an Adlerian inferiority complex, a repressed libido? Sometimes it is one, sometimes the other, depending on the story and the character. Faulkner often does not tell us. And, furthermore, this does not particularly interest him.

What matters to him is rather the *nature* of this new creature, a nature that is *poetic* and magical, full of manifold, but veiled, contradictions. This "nature"—what else can we call it?—which we grasp in terms of its psychological manifestations, does have a psychological existence. It is not even completely subconscious, since it often seems as if the men impelled by it can look back and contemplate it. But, on the other hand, it is fixed and immutable, like an evil spell. Faulkner's heroes bear it within them from the day of their birth.

It is as obstinate as stone or rock; it is *a thing*, a *spirit-thing*, an opaque, solidified spirit behind consciousness. It is a shadow, but a shadow whose essence is clarity—the magical object par excellence. Faulkner's creatures are bewitched, enveloped in a stifling atmosphere of witchcraft. That is what I meant by illusion. These spells are impossible. They are not even conceivable. And Faulkner takes care not to let us conceive them. His entire method aims at suggesting them.

Is he nothing more than an illusionist? I believe he is. Or, if not, he is tricking himself. There is a curious passage in *Sartoris* that provides us with the key to his deviousness and sincerity alike.

'Your Arlens and Sabatinis talk a lot, and nobody ever had more to say and more trouble saying it than old Dreiser.'

'But they have secrets,' she explained. 'Shakespeare doesn't have any secrets. He tells everything.'

'I see. Shakespeare had no sense of discrimination and no instinct for reticence. In other words, he wasn't a gentleman,' he suggested.

'Yes . . . That's what I mean.'

'And so, to be a gentleman, you must have secrets.'

'Oh, you make me tired.'

This dialogue is ambiguous and probably ironical. Narcissa is not very intelligent, and besides, Sabatini and Michael Arlen are bad writers. Yet, it seems to me that in this passage Faulkner reveals a good deal of himself. Though Narcissa may be somewhat lacking in literary taste, her instinct is sound in making her choose Bayard, a man who has secrets. Horace may be right in liking Shakespeare, but he is talkative and weak; he tells all, he is not a man. The men Faulkner likes—the negro in *Light in August*, the father in *Absalom*, Bayard Sartoris— are men who have secrets and keep quiet. Faulkner's humanism is probably the only acceptable kind. He hates our prattling, well-adjusted minds, our engineering mentality. But doesn't he realize that his great, dark figures are only façades? Is he taken in by his own art? He would probably not be satisfied by the repression of our secrets into the unconscious. He dreams of total darkness within consciousness itself, a total darkness that we ourselves make, within our very selves. This dream of silence, a silence outside us and a silence within us, is the futile dream of a puritan ultra-stoicism. Is he shamming? What does he do when he is alone? Does he put up with the endless prattle of his all too human consciousness? To know this, we would have to know Faulkner himself.

(February 1938)

VI

On "The Sound and the Fury"

Time in the Work of Faulkner

THE first thing that strikes one in reading *The Sound and the Fury* is its technical oddity. Why has Faulkner broken up the time of his story and scrambled the pieces? Why is the first window that opens out on this fictional world the consciousness of an idiot? The reader is tempted to look for guidemarks and to re-establish the chronology for himself:

Jason and Caroline Compson have had three sons and a daughter. The daughter, Caddy, has given herself to Dalton Ames and become pregnant by him. Forced to get hold of a husband quickly . . .

Here the reader stops, for he realizes he is telling another story. Faulkner did not first conceive this orderly plot so as to shuffle it afterwards like a pack of cards; he could not tell it in any other way. In the classical novel, action involves a central complication; for example, the murder of old Karamazov or the meeting of Edouard and Bernard in *The Coiners*. But we look in vain for such a complication in *The Sound and the Fury*. Is it the castration of Benjy or Caddy's wretched amorous adventure or Quentin's suicide or Jason's hatred of his niece? As soon as we begin to look at any episode, it opens up to reveal behind it other episodes, all the other episodes. Nothing happens; the story does not unfold; we discover it under each word, like an obscene and obstructing presence, more or less condensed, depending upon the particular case. It would be a mistake to regard these irregularities as gratuitous exercises in virtuosity. A fictional technique always relates back to the novelist's metaphysics. The critic's task is to define the latter before evaluating the former. Now, it is immediately obvious that Faulkner's metaphysics is a metaphysics of time.

Man's misfortune lies in his being time-bound.

. . . a man is the sum of his misfortunes. One day you'd think misfortune would get tired, but then time is your misfortune . . .

Such is the real subject of the book. And if the technique Faulkner has adopted seems at first a negation of temporality, the reason is that we confuse temporality with chronology. It was man who invented dates and clocks.

Constant speculation regarding the position of mechanical hands on an arbitrary dial which is a sympton of mind-function. Excrement Father said like sweating.

In order to arrive at real time, we must abandon this invented measure which is not a measure of anything.

. . . time is dead as long as it is being clicked off by little wheels; only when the clock stops does time come to life.

Thus, Quentin's gesture of breaking his watch has a symbolic value; it gives us access to a time without clocks. The time of Benjy, the idiot, who does not know how to tell time, is also clockless.

What is thereupon revealed to us is the present, and not the ideal limit whose place is neatly marked out between past and future. Faulkner's present is essentially catastrophic. It is the event which creeps up on us like a thief, huge, unthinkable—which creeps up on us and then disappears. Beyond this present time there is nothing, since the future does not exist. The present rises up from sources unknown to us and drives away another present; it is forever beginning anew. "And . . . and . . . and then." Like Dos Passos, but much more discreetly, Faulkner makes an accretion of his narrative. The actions themselves, even when seen by those who perform them, burst and scatter on entering the present.

I went to the dresser and took up the watch with the face still down. I tapped the crystal on the dresser and caught the fragments of glass in my hand and put them into the ashtray and twisted the hands off and put them in the tray. The watch ticked on.

The other aspect of this present is what I shall call a sinking in. I use this expression, for want of a better one, to indicate a kind of motionless movement of this formless monster. In Faulkner's work, there is never any progression, never anything which comes from the future. The present has not first been a future possibility, as when my friend, after having been *he for whom I am waiting*, finally appears. No, to be present means to appear without any reason and to sink in. This sinking in is not an abstract view. It is within things themselves that Faulkner perceives it and tries to make it felt.

The train swung around the curve, the engine puffing with short, heavy blasts, and they passed smoothly from sight that way, with that quality of shabby and timeless patience, of static serenity . . .

And again,

Beneath the sag of the buggy the hooves neatly rapid like motions of a lady doing embroidery, *diminishing without progress*[1] like a figure on a treadmill being drawn rapidly off-stage.

It seems as though Faulkner has laid hold of a frozen speed at the very heart of things; he is grazed by congealed spurts that wane and dwindle without moving.

This fleeting and unimaginable immobility can, however, be arrested and pondered. Quentin can say, "I broke my watch", but when he says it, his gesture is *past*. The past is named and related; it can, to a certain extent, be fixed by concepts or recognized by the heart. We pointed out earlier, in connection with *Sartoris*, that Faulkner always showed events when they were already over. In *The Sound and the Fury* everything has already happened. It is this that enables us to understand that strange remark by one of the heroes, "*Fui. Non sum.*" In this sense, too, Faulkner is able to make man a sum total without a future: "The sum of his climactic experiences", "The sum of his misfortunes", "The sum of what have you". At every moment, one draws a line, since the present is nothing but a chaotic din, a future that is past. Faulkner's vision of the world can be compared to that of a

[1] The author's *italics*.

man sitting in an open car and looking backwards. At every moment, formless shadows, flickerings, faint tremblings and patches of light rise up on either side of him, and only afterwards, when he has a little perspective, do they become trees and men and cars.

The past takes on a sort of super-reality; its contours are hard and clear, unchangeable. The present, nameless and fleeting, is helpless before it. It is full of gaps, and, through these gaps, things of the past, fixed, motionless and silent as judges or glances, come to invade it. Faulkner's monologues remind one of aeroplane trips full of air-pockets. At each pocket, the hero's consciousness "sinks back into the past" and rises only to sink back again. The present is not; it becomes. Everything *was*. In *Sartoris*, the past was called "the stories" because it was a matter of family memories that had been constructed, because Faulkner had not yet found his technique.

In *The Sound and the Fury* he is more individual and more undecided. But it is so strong an obsession that he is sometimes apt to disguise the present, and the present moves along in the shadow, like an underground river, and reappears only when it itself is past. When Quentin insults Blaid,[1] he is not even aware of doing so; he is reliving his dispute with Dalton Ames. And when Blaid punches his nose, this brawl is covered over and hidden by Quentin's past brawl with Ames. Later on, Shreve relates how Blaid hit Quentin; he relates this scene because it has become a story, but while it was unfolding in the present, it was only a furtive movement, covered over by veils. Someone once told me about an old monitor who had grown senile. His memory had stopped like a broken watch; it had been arrested at his fortieth year. He was sixty, but didn't know it. His last memory was that of a schoolyard and his daily walk around it. Thus, he interpreted his present in terms of his past and walked about his table, convinced that he was watching students during recreation.

Faulkner's characters are like that, only worse, for their past, which is in order, does not assume chronological order. It is, in actual fact, a matter of emotional constellations. Around a

[1] Compare the dialogue with Blaid inserted into the middle of the dialogue with Ames: "Did you ever have a sister?" etc., and the inextricable confusion of the two fights.

few central themes (Caddy's pregnancy, Benjy's castration, Quentin's suicide) gravitate innumerable silent masses. Whence the absurdity of the chronology of "the assertive and contradictory assurance" of the clock. The order of the past is the order of the heart. It would be wrong to think that when the present is past it becomes our closest memory. Its metamorphosis can cause it to sink to the bottom of our memory, just as it can leave it floating on the surface. Only its own density and the dramatic meaning of our life can determine at what level it will remain.

Such is the nature of Faulkner's time. Isn't there something familiar about it? This unspeakable present, leaking at every seam, these sudden invasions of the past, this emotional order, the opposite of the voluntary and intellectual order that is chronological but lacking in reality, these memories, these monstrous and discontinuous obsessions, these intermittences of the heart—are not these reminiscent of the lost and recaptured time of Marcel Proust? I am not unaware of the differences between the two; I know, for instance, that for Proust salvation lies in time itself, in the full reappearance of the past. For Faulkner, on the contrary, the past is never lost, unfortunately; it is always there, it is an obsession. One escapes from the temporal world only through mystic ecstasies. A mystic is always a man who wishes to forget something, his self or, more often, language or objective representations. For Faulkner, time must be forgotten.

'Quentin, I give you the mausoleum of all hope and desire; it's rather excruciatingly apt that you will use it to gain the reductio ad absurdum of all human experience which can fit your individual needs no better than it fitted his or his father's. I give it to you not that you may remember time, *but that you might forget it now and then for a moment* and not spend all your breath trying to conquer it. Because no battle is ever won he said. They are not even fought. The field only reveals to man his own folly and despair, and victory is an illusion of philosophers and fools.'

It is because he has forgotten time that the hunted negro in *Light in August* suddenly achieves his strange and horrible happiness.

It's not when you realize that nothing can help you—religion, pride, anything—it's when you realize that you don't need any aid.

But for Faulkner, as for Proust, time is, above all, *that which separates*. One recalls the astonishment of the Proustian heroes who can no longer enter into their past loves, of those lovers depicted in *Les Plaisirs et Les Jours*, clutching their passions, afraid they will pass and knowing they will. We find the same anguish in Faulkner.

. . . people cannot do anything very dreadful at all, they cannot even remember tomorrow what seemed dreadful today . . .

and

. . . a love or a sorrow is a bond purchased without design and which matures willynilly and is recalled without warning to be replaced by whatever issue the gods happen to be floating at the time . . .

To tell the truth, Proust's fictional technique *should have been* Faulkner's. It was the logical conclusion of his metaphysics. But Faulkner is a lost man, and it is because he feels lost that he takes risks and pursues his thought to its uttermost consequences. Proust is a Frenchman and a classicist. The French lose themselves only a little at a time and always manage to find themselves again. Eloquence, intellectuality and a liking for clear ideas were responsible for Proust's retaining at least the semblance of chronology.

The basic reason for this relationship is to be found in a very general literary phenomenon. Most of the great contemporary authors, Proust, Joyce, Dos Passos, Faulkner, Gide and Virginia Woolf have tried, each in his own way, to distort time. Some of them have deprived it of its past and future in order to reduce it to the pure intuition of the instant; others, like Dos Passos, have made of it a dead and closed memory. Proust and Faulkner have simply decapitated it. They have deprived it of its future, that is, its dimension of deeds and freedom. Proust's heroes never undertake anything. They do, of course, make plans, but their plans remain stuck to them and cannot be projected like a bridge beyond the present. They are day-dreams that are put to flight by reality. The

Albertine who appears is not the one we were expecting, and the expectation was merely a slight, inconsequential hesitation, limited to the moment only. As to Faulkner's heroes, they never look ahead. They face backwards as the car carries them along. The coming suicide which casts its shadow over Quentin's last day is not a human possibility; not for a second does Quentin envisage the possibility of *not* killing himself. This suicide is an immobile wall, a *thing* which he approaches backwards, and which he neither wants to nor can conceive.

. . . you seem to regard it merely as an experience that will whiten your hair overnight so to speak without altering your appearance at all . . .

It is not an *undertaking*, but a fatality. In losing its element of possibility it ceases to exist in the future. It is already present, and Faulkner's entire art aims at suggesting to us that Quentin's monologues and his last walk *are already* his suicide. This, I think, explains the following curious paradox: Quentin thinks of his last day in the past, like someone who is remembering. But in that case, since the hero's last thoughts coincide approximately with the bursting of his memory and its annihilation, who is remembering? The inevitable reply is that the novelist's skill consists in the choice of the present moment from which he narrates the past. And Faulkner, like Salacrou in *L'Inconnu d'Arras*, has chosen the infinitesimal instant of death. Thus, when Quentin's memory begins to unravel its recollections ("Through the wall I heard Shreve's bed-springs and then his slippers on the floor hishing. I got up . . .") *he is already dead*. All this artistry and, to speak frankly, all this illusion are meant, then, merely as substitutions for the intuition of the future lacking in the author himself. This explains everything, particularly the irrationality of time; since the present is the unexpected, the formless can be determined only by an excess of memories. We now also understand why duration is "man's characteristic misfortune". If the future has reality, time withdraws us from the past and brings us nearer to the future; but if you do away with the future, time is no longer that which separates, that which cuts the present off from itself. "You cannot bear to think that someday it will no longer hurt you like this." Man spends his life struggling against time, and time, like an acid, eats away at man, eats him away from himself and prevents him from fulfilling his human character. Everything is absurd. "Life is a tale told by an idiot, full of sound and fury, signifying nothing."

But is man's time without a future? I can understand that the nail's time, or the clod's or the atom's is a perpetual present. But is man a thinking nail? If you begin by plunging him into universal time, the time of planets and nebulae, of tertiary flexures and animal species, as into a bath of sulphuric acid, then the question is settled. However, a consciousness buffeted so from one instant to another ought, *first of all*, to be a consciousness and then, *afterwards*, to be temporal; does anyone believe that time can come to it from the outside? Consciousness can "exist within time" only on condition that it become time as a result of the very movement by which it becomes consciousness. It must become "temporalized", as Heidegger says. We can no longer arrest man at each present and define him as "the sum of what he has". The nature of consciousness implies, on the contrary, that it project itself into the future. We can understand what it is only through what it will be. It is determined in its present being by its own possibilities. This is what Heidegger calls "the silent force of the possible". You will not recognize within yourself Faulkner's man, a creature bereft of possibilities and explicable only in terms of what he has been. Try to pin down your consciousness and probe it. You will see that it is hollow. In it you will find only the future.

I do not even speak of your plans and expectations. But the very gesture that you catch in passing has meaning for you only if you project its fulfilment out of it, out of yourself, into the not-yet. This very cup, with its bottom that you do not see —that you might see, that is, at the end of a movement you have not yet made—this white sheet of paper, whose underside is hidden (but you could turn over the sheet) and all the stable and bulky objects that surround us display their most immediate and densest qualities in the future. Man is not the sum of what he has, but the totality of what he does not yet have, of what he might have. And if we steep ourselves thus in the future, is not the formless brutality of the present thereby attenuated? The single event does not spring on us like a thief, since it is, by nature, a Having-been-future. And if a historian wishes to explain the past, must he not first seek out its future? I am afraid that the absurdity that Faulkner finds in a human life is one that he himself has put there. Not that life is not absurd, but there is another kind of absurdity.

Why have Faulkner and so many other writers chosen this particular absurdity which is so un-novelistic and so untrue? I think we should have to look for the reason in the social conditions of our present life. Faulkner's despair seems to me to precede his metaphysics. For him, as for all of us, the future is closed. Everything we see and experience impels us to say, "This can't last." And yet change is not even conceivable, except in the form of a cataclysm. We are living in a time of impossible revolutions, and Faulkner uses his extraordinary art to describe our suffocation and a world dying of old age. I like his art, but I do not believe in his metaphysics. A closed future is still a future. "Even if human reality has nothing more 'before' it, even if 'its account is closed', its being is still determined by this 'self-anticipation'. The loss of all hope, for example, does not deprive human reality of its possibilities; it is simply a way of *being* toward these same possibilities."[1]

(July 1939)

---

[1] Heidegger, *Zein und Zeit*.

VII

John Dos Passos and "1919"

A NOVEL is a mirror. So everyone says. But what is meant by *reading* a novel? It means, I think, jumping into the mirror. You suddenly find yourself on the other side of the glass, among people and objects that have a familiar look. But they merely look familiar. We have never really seen them. The things of our world have, in turn, become outside reflections. You close the book, step over the edge of the mirror and return to this honest-to-goodness world, and you find furniture, gardens and people who have nothing to say to you. The mirror that closed behind you reflects them peacefully, and now you would swear that art is a reflection. There are clever people who go so far as to talk of distorting mirrors.

Dos Passos very consciously uses this absurd and insistent illusion to impel us to revolt. He had done everything possible to make his novel seem a mere reflection. He has even donned the garb of populism. The reason is that his art is not gratuitous; he wants to prove something. But observe what a curious aim he has. He wants to show us this world, our own—to *show* it only, without explanations or comment. There are no revelations about the machinations of the police, the imperialism of the oil kings or the Ku-Klux-Klan, no cruel pictures of poverty. We have already seen everything he wants to show us, and, so it seems at first glance, seen it exactly as he wants us to see it. We recognize immediately the sad abundance of these untragic lives. They are our own lives, these innumerable, planned, botched, immediately forgotten and constantly renewed adventures that slip by without leaving a trace, without involving anyone, until the time when one of them, no different from any of the others, suddenly, as if through some clumsy trickery, sickens a man for good and throws a mechanism out of gear.

Now, it is by depicting, as we ourselves might depict, these too familiar appearances with which we all put up that Dos Passos makes them unbearable. He arouses indignation in people who never get indignant, he frightens people who fear nothing. But hasn't there been some sleight-of-hand? I look about me and see people, cities, boats, the war. But they aren't the real thing; they are discreetly queer and sinister, as in a nightmare. My indignation against this world also seems dubious to me; it only faintly resembles the other indignation, the kind that a mere news item can arouse. I am on the other side of the mirror.

Dos Passos' hate, despair and lofty contempt are real. But that is precisely why his world is not real; it is a created object. I know of none—not even Faulkner's or Kafka's—in which the art is greater or better hidden. I know of none that is more precious, more touching or closer to us. This is because he takes his material from our world. And yet, there is no stranger or more distant world. Dos Passos has invented only one thing, an art of story-telling. But that is enough to create a universe.

We live in time, we calculate in time. The novel, like life, unfolds in the present. The perfect tense exists on the surface only; it must be interpreted as a present *with aesthetic distance*, as a stage device. In the novel the dice are not loaded, for fictional man is free. He develops before our eyes; our impatience, our ignorance, our expectancy are the same as the hero's. The tale, on the other hand, as Fernandez has shown, develops in the past. But the tale explains. Chronological order, life's order, barely conceals the causal order, which is an order for the understanding. The event does not touch us; it stands half-way between fact and law. Dos Passos' time is his own creation; it is neither fictional nor narrative. It is rather, if you like, historical time. The perfect and imperfect tenses are not used simply to observe the rules; the reality of Joe's or of Eveline's adventures lies in the fact they are now part of the past. Everything is told as if by someone who is remembering.

'*The years Dick was little* he never heard anything about his Dad . . .' 'All Eveline thought about *that winter* was going to the Art Institute . . .' 'They waited two weeks in Vigo while the officials quarrelled about their status and they got pretty fed up with it.'

The fictional event is a nameless presence; there is nothing one can say about it, for it develops. We may be shown two men combing a city for their mistresses, but we are not told that they "do not find them", for this is not true. So long as there remains one street, one café, one house to explore, it is not yet true. In Dos Passos, the things that happen are named first, and then the dice are cast, as they are in our memories.

Glen and Joe only got ashore for a few hours and couldn't find Marcelline and Loulou.

The facts are clearly outlined; they are ready for *thinking about*. But Dos Passos never thinks them. Not for an instant does the order of causality betray itself in chronological order. There is no narrative, but rather the jerky unreeling of a rough and uneven memory, which sums up a period of several years in a few words only to dwell languidly over a minute fact. Like our real memories, it is a jumble of miniatures and frescoes. There is relief enough, but it is cunningly scattered at random. One step further would give us the famous idiot's monologue in *The Sound and the Fury*. But that would still involve intellectualizing, suggesting an explanation in terms of the irrational, suggesting a Freudian order beneath this disorder. Dos Passos stops just in time. As a result of this, past things retain a flavour of the present; they still remain, in their exile, what they once were, inexplicable tumults of colour, sound and passion. Each event is irreducible, a gleaming and solitary *thing* that does not flow from anything else, but suddenly arises to join other things. For Dos Passos, narrating means adding. This accounts for the slack air of his style. "And ... and ... and ..." The great disturbing phenomena—war, love, political movements, strikes—fade and crumble into an infinity of little odds and ends which can just about be set side by side. Here is the armistice:

In early November rumours of an armistice began to fly around and then suddenly one afternoon Major Wood ran into the office that Eleanor and Eveline shared and dragged them both away from their desks and kissed them both and shouted, "At last it's come." Before she knew it Eveline found herself kissing Major

Moorehouse right on the mouth. The Red Cross office turned into a college dormitory the night of a football victory: It was the Armistice.

Everybody seemed suddenly to have bottles of cognac and to be singing, *There's a long long trail awinding* or *La Made-lon pour nous n'est pas sévère.*

These Americans see war the way Fabrizio saw the battle of Waterloo. And the intention, like the method, is clear upon reflection. But you must close the book and reflect.

Passions and gestures are also things. Proust analysed them, related them to former states and thereby made them inevitable. Dos Passos wants to retain only their factual nature. All he is allowed to say is, "In that place and at that time Richard was that way, and at another time, he was different." Love and decisions are great spheres that rotate on their own axes. The most we can grasp is a kind of *conformity* between the psychological state and the exterior situation, something resembling a colour harmony. We may also suspect that explanations are *possible*, but they seem as frivolous and futile as a spider-web on a heavy red flower. Yet, never do we have the feeling of fictional freedom: Dos Passos imposes upon us instead the unpleasant impression of an indeterminacy of detail. Acts, emotions and ideas suddenly settle within a character, make themselves at home and then disappear without his having much to say in the matter. You cannot say he submits to them. He experiences them. There seems to be no law governing their appearance.

Nevertheless, they once did exist. This lawless past is irremediable. Dos Passos has purposely chosen the perspective of history to tell a story. He wants to make us feel that the stakes are down. In *Man's Hope*, Malraux says, more or less, that "the tragic thing about death is that it transforms life into a destiny". With the opening lines of his book, Dos Passos settles down into death. The lives he tells about are all closed in on themselves. They resemble those Bergsonian memories which, after the body's death, float about, lifeless and full of odours and lights and cries, through some forgotten limbo. We constantly have the feeling that these vague, human lives are destinies. Our own past is not at all like this. There is not one of our acts whose meaning and value we cannot still transform even now. But beneath the violent colours of these beautiful, motley objects that Dos Passos presents there is something petrified. Their significance is fixed. Close your eyes and try to remember your own life, try to remember it *that way*; you will stifle. It is this unrelieved stifling that Dos Passos wanted to express. In capitalist society, men do not have lives, they have only destinies. He never says this, but he makes it felt throughout. He expresses it discreetly, cautiously, until we feel like smashing our destinies. We have become rebels; he has achieved his purpose.

We are rebels *behind the looking-glass*. For that is not what the rebel of this world wants to change. He wants to transform Man's *present* condition, the one that develops day by day. Using the past tense to tell about the present means using a device, creating a strange and beautiful world, as frozen as one of those Mardi-Gras masks that become frightening on the faces of real, living men.

But whose memories are these that unfold through the novel? At first glance, they seem to be those of the heroes, of Joe, Dick, Fillette and Eveline. And, on occasion, they are. As a rule, whenever a character is sincere, whenever he is bursting with something, no matter how, or with what:

When he went off duty he'd walk home achingly tired through the strawberry-scented early Parisian morning, thinking of the faces and the eyes and the sweat-drenched hair and the clenched fingers clotted with blood and dirt . . .

But the narrator often ceases to coincide completely with the hero. The hero could not quite have said what he does say, but you feel a discreet complicity between them. The narrator relates from the outside what the hero would have wanted him to relate. By means of this complicity, Dos Passos, without warning us, has us make the transition he was after. We suddenly find ourselves inside a horrible memory whose every recollection makes us uneasy, a bewildering memory that is no longer that of either the characters or the author. It seems like a chorus that remembers, a sententious chorus that is accessory to the deed.

All the same he got along very well at school and the teachers liked him, particularly Miss Teazle, the English teacher, because he had nice manners and said little things that weren't fresh but that made them laugh. Miss Teazle said he showed real feeling for English composition. One Christmas he sent her a little rhyme he made up about the Christ Child and the three Kings and she declared he had a gift.

The narration takes on a slightly stilted manner, and everything that is reported about the hero assumes the solemn quality of a public announcement: " . . . she declared he had a gift". The sentence is not accompanied by any comment, but acquires a sort of collective resonance. It is a *declaration*. And indeed, whenever we want to know his characters' thoughts, Dos Passos, with respectful objectivity, generally gives us their declarations.

Fred . . . said the last night before they left he was going to tear loose. When they got to the front he might get killed and then what? Dick said he liked talking to the girls but that the whole business was too commercial and turned his stomach. Ed Schuyler, who'd been nicknamed Frenchie and was getting very continental in his ways, said that the street girls were too naive.

I open *Paris-Soir* and read, *"From our special correspondent: Charlie Chaplin declares that he has put an end to Charlie."* Now I have it! Dos Passos reports all his characters' utterances to us in the style of a statement to the Press. Their words are thereby cut off from thought, and become pure utterances, simple reactions that must be registered as such, in the behaviourist style upon which Dos Passos draws when it suits him to do so. But, at the same time, the utterance takes on a social importance; it is inviolable, it becomes a maxim. Little does it matter, thinks the satisfied chorus, what Dick had in mind when he spoke that sentence. What matters is that it has been uttered. Besides, it was not formed inside him, it came from afar. Even before he uttered it, it existed as a pompous sound, a taboo. All he has done is to lend it his power of affirmation. It is as if there were a Platonic heaven of words and commonplaces to which we all go to find words suitable to a given situation. There is a heaven of gestures, too. Dos Passos makes a pretence of presenting gestures as pure events, as mere exteriors, as free, animal movements. But this is only appearance. Actually, in relating them, he adopts the point of view of the chorus, of public opinion. There is no single one of Dick's or of Eleanor's gestures which is not a public demonstration, performed to a humming accompaniment of flattery.

At Chantilly they went through the château and fed the big carp in the moat. They ate their lunch in the woods, sitting on rubber cushions. J.W. kept everybody laughing explaining how he hated picnics, asking everybody what it was that got into even the most intelligent women that they were always trying to make people go on picnics. After lunch they drove out to Senlis to see the houses that the Uhlans had destroyed there in the battle of the Marne.

Doesn't it sound like a local newspaper's account of an ex-servicemen's banquet? All of a sudden, as the gesture dwindles until it is no more than a thin film, we see that it *counts*, that it is sacred in character and that, at the same time, it involves commitment. But for whom? For the abject consciousness of "everyman", for what Heidegger calls "das Mann". But still, where does it spring from? Who is its representative as I read? *I* am. In order to understand the words, in order to make sense out of the paragraphs, I first have to adopt his point of view. I have to play the role of the obliging chorus. This consciousness exists only through me; without me there would be nothing but black spots on white paper. But even while I *am* this collective consciousness, I want to wrench away from it, to see it from the judge's point of view, that is, to get free of myself. This is the source of the shame and uneasiness with which Dos Passos knows how to fill the reader. I am a reluctant accomplice (though I am not even sure that I am reluctant), creating and rejecting social taboos. I am, deep in my heart, a revolutionary again, an unwilling one.

In return, how I hate Dos Passos' men! I am given a fleeting glimpse of their minds, just enough to see that they are living animals. Then, they begin to unwind their endless tissue of ritual statements and sacred gestures. For them, there is no break between inside and outside, between body and consciousness, but only between the stammerings of an individual's timid, intermittent, fumbling thinking and the messy world of

collective representations. What a simple process this is, and
how effective! All one need do is use American journalistic
technique in telling the story of a life, and like the Salzburg
reed, a life crystallizes into the Social, and the problem of the
transition to the typical—stumbling-block of the social novel—
is thereby resolved. There is no further need to present a
working man type, to compose (as Nizan does in *Antoine
Bloyé*) an existence which represents the exact average of
thousands of existences. Dos Passos, on the contrary, can give
all his attention to rendering a single life's special character.
Each of his characters is unique; what happens to him could
happen to no one else. What does it matter, since Society has
marked him more deeply than could any special circumstance,
since *he is* Society? Thus, we get a glimpse of an order beyond
the accidents of fate or the contingency of detail, an order more
supple than Zola's physiological necessity or Proust's psychological mechanism, a soft and insinuating constraint which
seems to release its victims, letting them go only to take
possession of them again without their suspecting, in other
words, a statistical determinism. These men, submerged in their
own existences, live as they can. They struggle; what comes
their way is not determined in advance. And yet, neither their
efforts, their faults, nor their most extreme violence can inter-
fere with the regularity of births, marriages and suicides. The
pressure exerted by a gas on the walls of its container does not
depend upon the individual histories of the molecules compos-
ing it.

We are still on the other side of the looking-glass. Yesterday
you saw your best friend and expressed to him your passionate
hatred of war. Now try to relate this conversation to yourself
in the style of Dos Passos. "And they ordered two beers and
said that war was hateful. Paul declared he would rather do
anything than fight and John said he agreed with him and both
got excited and said they were glad they agreed. On his way
home, Paul decided to see John more often." You will start
hating yourself immediately. It will not take you long, however, to decide that you *cannot* use this tone in talking about
yourself. However insincere you may have been, you were at
least living out your insincerity, playing it out on your own,
continuously creating and extending its existence from one

moment to the next. And even if you got caught up in collective representations, you had first to experience them as personal resignation. We are neither mechanical objects nor possessed souls, but something worse; we are free. We exist either entirely *within* or entirely *without*. Dos Passos' man is a hybrid creature, an interior-exterior being. We go on living with him and within him, with his vacillating, individual consciousness, when suddenly it wavers, weakens, and is diluted in the collective consciousness. We follow it up to that point and suddenly, before we notice, we are on the outside. The man behind the looking-glass is a strange, contemptible, fascinating creature. Dos Passos knows how to use this constant shifting to fine effect. I know of nothing more gripping than Joe's death.

Joe laid out a couple of frogs and was backing off towards the door, when he saw in the mirror that a big guy in a blouse was bringing down a bottle on his head held with both hands. He tried to swing around but he didn't have time. The bottle crashed his skull and he was out.

We are inside with him, until the shock of the bottle on his skull. Then immediately, we find ourselves outside with the chorus, part of the collective memory, ". . . and he was out." Nothing gives you a clearer feeling of annihilation. And from then on, each page we turn, each page that tells of other minds and of a world going on without Joe, is like a spadeful of earth over our bodies. But it is a behind-the-looking-glass death: all we really get is the fine *appearance* of nothingness. True nothingness can neither be felt nor thought. Neither you nor I, nor anyone after us, will ever have anything to say about our real deaths.

Dos Passos' world—like those of Faulkner, Kafka and Stendhal—is impossible because it is contradictory. But therein lies its beauty. Beauty is a veiled contradiction. I regard Dos Passos as the greatest writer of our time.

(*August* 1938.)